Heartprints of God

The Early Years

By Stacy L. Sanchez

Heartprints of God
The Early Years

By Stacy L. Sanchez

ISBN: 978-1-7326327-5-2

Contents

A Divine Appointment

It was late.
I was tired.
My husband and I
both hungry.

As I drove out
of the parking lot,
I phoned my husband
to tell him
I would soon be home.

As we discussed
"dinner plans",
it was decided take out
was our best option and me,
the best one to pick it up
since I was already out.

I soon found myself
at a local sandwich shop.

After placing our order,
I took a nearby seat
and began the process
of waiting.

All I could think of
was getting home,
eating,

and going to bed.

My thoughts were soon
interrupted
by the voice
of an irate customer.

Her complaints were trivial.
Obviously her tirade
was more about
drawing attention to herself
than to her order.

The young lady
assisting her
was amazing.

Through all the
verbal abuse,
unreasonable complaints
and demands
placed on her
by this customer,
her countenance
never changed.

Her smile remained
and her voice was calm
and remarkably pleasant.

As I sat there
witnessing this scene,
I felt impressed by God
to commend this young lady
for her professionalism.

As soon as
my number was called
and my order ready,

A Divine Appointment

I would approach her
at the counter
and pass along words
of much deserved praise
and recognition.

Impressed by the behavior
of this young lady,
my eyes continued
to follow her
as she worked.

After completing an order,
she headed to the phone
and began to call someone.

I couldn't help
overhearing
her conversation.

Evidently, no one
had shown up
to babysit
her young children
and they were home alone.

It was quite obvious
she had made
several earlier calls,
just like this one,
in hopes of locating
someone to watch over
her little ones
until her shift ended
and she could return home.

From the look
on her face,
this phone call

only brought with it
another
"No, I'm sorry I can't"
along with mounting fear
for her children.

As she hung up,
she sat in a chair,
rubbing her forehead
with one hand
while wiping tears
with her other.

My number was called
and I approached
the counter
to pick up our order.

I had been waiting
for this moment
to speak with her,
but now,
she was sitting
in the back portion
of the kitchen.

Silently I prayed
the Lord would give me
the opportunity.

She looked up
and surprisingly,
I was able
to catch her eye
with the wave
of my hand.

She smiled
and made her way

A Divine Appointment

to the counter.

"Yes?
How can I help you?
Is there something wrong
with your order?" she asked,
trying to hide
the fear in her heart
and the tears in her eyes.

"No." I replied.
"I just couldn't
leave here tonight
without telling you
how much I appreciate
the professional
and kind manner
in which you dealt
with that difficult customer
earlier.

I know it
wasn't easy
for you.

God provided you
with the inner strength
you needed.

He is always
right here with you,
and just like
He gave you the strength
to deal with that woman,
He will give you the strength
to deal with whatever
may be happening
in your life
right at this very moment.

He cares for you
and He will be faithful
to provide you
with all you need.
I will be praying for you"

She smiled,
thanked me,
and handed me
my order.

I walked
in the direction
of the door
and she
returned to her work.

As I reached my car,
I bowed my head
in prayer.

As I had watched
in disgust,
the behavior of the
self-absorbed customer,
God had opened my eyes
to see my own
selfishness
reflected through her actions.

How my "I"-rate behavior
must disgust
my Heavenly Father!

Lord, forgive me.

As I had watched
the beauty
of the young lady serving,

A Divine Appointment

I had seen my own need
for more of Christ
in my heart and life.

Lord, live in and through me.

As I had glimpsed
the deeply hidden anguish
in this young woman's life,
I had been reminded
to speak more kinder
and treat others more gently,
for we never know
what they may be facing
in their lives.

Lord, teach me to love.

As I was given
the privilege to speak
words of affirmation
and encouragement
to this hurting heart,
I was convicted
to seek out
every door of opportunity
to share words
of hope, love and truth
with those around me.

Lord, use me to speak your words to others.

As I drove home,
I realized
I was no longer
feeling upset,
tired and fatigued.

Instead, I felt refreshed!
I prayed the young lady
at the sandwich shop
felt refreshed, too!

Purpose to Pray

Today I am wearing
one of my favorite
pairs of shoes,
my Miranda shoes.

No,
Miranda is not
a famous designer
of footwear,
although she might
grow up
to be one someday.

Miranda is a
former student
of mine,
and the shoes,
a constant reminder
for me
to pray for her.

Let me explain.

Miranda was an
excellent student
and learning
came easy for this
energetic,
independent 3rd grader.

Easy in every subject
except Math,
that is.

For some reason,
Miranda struggled
with mathematical concepts.

The only thing
that came easy
for Miranda
during Math class
was frustration!

So,
at the first
parent-teacher conference
of the school year,
I offered
to tutor Miranda
each day after school,
at no cost
to the family.

Her mother
willingly accepted
my invitation,
and the tutoring began.

The school year
flew by quickly
and I was proud
of the progress
Miranda had made.

At an Educational Fair
held the final week of school,
I was approached
by Miranda's grandmother.

She gently
squeezed my arm,
smiled,
and handed me
an envelope.

Then,
she slipped
into the crowd
gathered in the gym
to view the various
projects and exhibits
on display.

That evening,
I opened
the envelope
to find a
beautiful,
handwritten note
thanking me
for tutoring
her precious granddaughter.

To further show
her appreciation,
she had enclosed
a check.

A few months later,
while shopping
at a local mall,
I came across
a pair of black shoes.

I had been wanting
to replace
my old ones
and these were just

what I had been
looking for.

I tried them on
and they fit
perfectly.

There was only one problem.

Our budget was tight
and I didn't have
any extra money
to spend on them.

Then,
I remembered
Miranda
and the generosity
of her grandmother.

Months earlier,
when I had
cashed her check,
my husband had told me
to tuck the money
into a "hidden" place
in my wallet
so it would be there
when I wanted
to buy
something special.

Money in hand,
I headed to the
check out counter.

As I waited in line
to purchase
my shoes,

Purpose to Pray

I thanked God
for the money
I had received.

Then,
I smiled
and prayed
a special prayer
just for Miranda.

These shoes,
in a roundabout way,
had brought
Miranda
to my mind
and a prayer for her
to my lips!

At that moment,
I purposed
in my heart
to say a prayer
for Miranda
each and every time
I put on
my "Miranda shoes".

I also purposed
to pray for others
in my life,
every time
I saw something
that made me
think of them.

How many times
has something
in your day
made you think

of a family member
or a close friend?

While driving to work
you see a car
that looks identical
to the one
your friend drives.

While eating
at a restaurant,
your waitress
has the same name
as your aunt.

While watching
the evening news,
you hear the name
of the town
your friend lives in.

Are these simply coincidences?

I don't think so.

God has given us
the unique privilege
and the awesome
responsibility
to pray for others.

So,
this morning
as I put on
my Miranda shoes,
I prayed
for precious Miranda.

Purpose to Pray

A couple of days ago,
when I received
an email
from a special friend,
I prayed for her.

This morning,
when I saw
a little girl
who reminded me
of my own sister
at that young age,
I prayed for her.

Yesterday,
while shopping for groceries,
I saw a pregnant lady,
and prayed for a friend of mine
who is expecting
a little one of her own.

How humbling and exciting
to remember our God
can use ordinary things
in our lives
to do *extraordinary* things
in the lives of others
when we allow ourselves
to be used by Him
to pray for someone in need.

Today,
why not purpose
in your heart
to pray
whenever God chooses
to use you?

Faith is the Key

Sally had done it now.

With one step
of her little black paw
on the front door lock,
she had locked herself
inside the car,
and worse of all,
had locked me out.

To make matters worse,
the engine was still on,
and now in this new situation,
my fear and anxiety
had turned on, too!

What a sight
we must have been.

An excited little puppy
pouncing on the inside
of the door,
looking out the window
at me,
while I stood there,
a helpless grown adult,
looking in at her!

Faith is the Key

It had all started
when I decided
to stop and check my mail
at the group of mailboxes
located at the end
of our cul-de-sac.

It was mid-July.

With temperatures over
the 100 degree mark,
I had opted
to leave the car running
with the air conditioner on.

I hopped out of the car,
with only the mailbox key
in my hand.

When I returned back to the car
and reached for the door handle,
Sally excitedly jumped up
on the door to greet me
and had inadvertently
created a chasm
as deep as the Grand Canyon
between us.

What could I do now?

Pray, of course,
and pray I did.

Instantly, the thought came to me:
*The key to unlock the door
is right in your hand.*

But as quickly
as this thought had come,

doubts had come, too,
rising to the forefront
of my mind,
drowning it out.

That key will never fit
in the lock
for the car door.
It's just a mailbox key.
Why sometimes
it's even a struggle
to get it to fit
in the mailbox lock.
Open a car door?
Nope, it will never work.

I decided
to walk
around the car
and check
the doors and windows.

Maybe I would
find one of the
other three doors
had been left unlocked.
Perhaps a window
might be opened
just enough
to aid me
in solving
this unfortunate dilemma.

But,
after checking
each door and window
at least twice,
I was the one
still standing outside the car,

anxious, frantic and hot,
while my puppy
was the one on the inside,
calm, cool, and collected.

Repeatedly,
the same thought-
The key to unlock the door
is right in your hand,-
kept trying to push
its way through
the crowd of doubt
and self-reliance
flooding my mind.

Ridiculous.
Absurd.
It will never work.
There has to be
something else
I can do.
But what?

What could I do?

I kept trying
to think of a way
to get into my car,
while stubbornly
refusing to listen
to His still small voice.

Finally,
after what seemed
like an eternity,
I decided to "give in"
and try the mailbox key.

After all,
what would it hurt?
I could at least try
to use this key
to open the door,
couldn't I?

So,
slowly and
almost reverently,
I inserted
the mailbox key
into the keyhole........
and it
turned.

The door lock
popped up
and the wall
between Sally and I
came tumbling down.

How I could
have saved myself
these past minutes
of tension,
frustration
and sweat!

The answer
to my problem
had come as soon
as I had prayed.

The Lord
had been faithful
to send help
the moment
I had needed it.

I was the one
who delayed.
I was the one
who hindered
His assistance
by my pride
and a spirit
of self-reliance.

Truly,
the key
to unlock the door
had been
right in my hand
the whole time.

How often we come
face to face
with locked doors
in our lives.

A rejection by a spouse.
A pink slip from our employer.
A rebellious child.
A life threatening illness.

We see no earthly way
of unlocking this door,
so we stand
helplessly
on the outside
looking in.

We plead with God
to help us,
and when His answer comes,
we choose our own solutions
which seem more logical,
and more reasonable,

only to find
they are unsuccessful and futile.

God whispers
His direction and guidance
time and time again.

The key to unlock the door
is right in your hand.

And so it is.
For God has given
to each of us
a measure of faith,
and it is faith alone
that is needed
to unlock these doors
in our lives.

A few weeks later,
my curiosity
got the best of me.

I kept wondering
if God had truly
worked a miracle
in my behalf,
or if that mailbox key
was just similar enough
to that of the car key
that it had worked when tried.

Once again,
with the same reverence
as before,
I slowly approached my car
and tried to insert
the very same mailbox key
into the lock.

Faith is the Key

This time,
to my surprise,
it wouldn't even begin
to go in the lock,
much less
unlock the door.

But then again,
why should it?
That key, after all,
is just a simple mailbox key
whose only purpose
is to allow me access
to my mailbox
so I can retrieve my mail.

Nothing more.
Nothing less.

Faith is what
unlocked
my car door!

Eyes Wide Open

Plans for a peaceful end
to a relaxing day
came to a screeching halt
when my husband
came to a sudden stop
while driving up our driveway.

There in plain sight,
soaking up the heat
from our concrete drive,
was a snake.

If *I* had been the one
behind the wheel,
not only would
forward progress
have stopped,
but backward progress
would have started
immediately!

Our new guest,
although uninvited,
had obviously seen the
"Mi Casa es Su Casa" plaque
above our front door
and had decided
to take us up
on the offer.

Actually,
we have no such sign,
but I don't think
that bothered
this slithery creature.

It was just
a matter of time
before it
would be hanging up
a sign of it's own;
one that would read,
"Home sweet Home."

Needless to say,
we were not excited
about this new addition.

My husband
bravely and cautiously
stepped out of our vehicle
and walked toward
the front of our car.

I chose to let my eyes
do the walking for me,
while the rest of my body
stayed belted in
the passenger seat,
safe and secure.

Expecting to meet
this guest
face to face,
my husband was
surprised to discover
it had made tracks
and was now
on the move.

Out of the corner
of his eye,
he caught a glimpse
of the tail end
of this serpent
as it slipped into
the nearby bushes.

The snake vanished quickly,
taking our peace of mind with it.

For the rest of the summer,
life as normal
could not be found
at our home
as long as
our new visitor
kept eluding us.

Now,
each time
we stepped outdoors,
this creature was the first
and oftentimes,
the only thing
on our mind.

It was out there.
We knew it.
We just didn't know
where it would show up next.

We had been surprised
by this creature once
and didn't want to be
caught unaware
a second time.

Eyes Wide Open

Taking out the garbage,
which "pre-snake"
was a nice excuse
to venture outside,
had now turned into
a mad dash out
and a mad dash back in.

No time to stop
and smell the roses
when our new guest
might be somewhere
tiptoeing through the tulips!

Nights of sitting out
on our patio
gazing at the stars
were replaced with nights
of sitting on our couch
watching TV
and staring at "stars"
far less inspiring.

Our garage door,
which we usually
left slightly ajar
during the hot days
of summer,
was now locked down
tighter than Fort Knox.

Each time life
took us outside
the safety of our home,
our eyes would quickly
begin their job
of meticulously scouring the yard
for any sign of the snake.

Thankfully,
we never did see
our yard guest again.

From the way
we were acting,
you would have thought
we had never seen
a snake before.

Snakes,
however,
are not an oddity
where we live.

Here,
in the southwestern
part of New Mexico,
they are almost
as common
as a cactus
or a tumbleweed.

What was odd
was our
total complacency
toward this
known danger
prior to
our snake siting.

Living with a
new heightened
level of security
that summer
got me thinking.

Like the snake,
Satan is a

known danger
in my life.

The Bible warns
I need to always
be on guard
so this enemy
of my soul
will not catch me
unaware.

Yet,
how easily
I let my guard down,
forgetting
this original serpent
can show up
at any time
and any place
in my Christian walk.

How often
I leave myself
vulnerable for attack
by neglecting
to fortify my heart
with God's words
of hope and promise.

How carelessly
I step out into my life
without first
focusing my eyes
on my Saviour
and scouring
my heart and life
for signs of spiritual danger.

Foolishly,
I allow myself
to become complacent,
living my life
totally oblivious
to Satan,
who is
ever seeking
to devour me.

Yes,
the snake who sought
to take up residence
in our yard that summer
and the serpent
who is constantly looking
for any opportunity
to move into my heart
are very similar indeed.

However,
despite their
obvious similarities,
there remains one
striking difference.

The snake meant
no intentional harm.
Satan does.

Even more reason
for me to be
sober and vigilant
and to keep the eyes
of my heart
wide open!

Fully Satisfied

As I was paying the cashier
for the gas I had just
pumped into my car,
I was approached
by a young man
in his early twenties.

"Excuse me, Ma'am.
Is that your
little green Honda?" he asked.

Not sure who he was
or why he was interested
in my little green Honda,
I apprehensively answered, "Yes."

"Did you just fill up
at that pump?" he asked next.

"Yes, I used that pump,
although I didn't fill up.
I only purchased
about eight gallons.
Why do you ask?"

"Well, I used that
very same pump
right before you
and I did fill up.

31

It cost me over $50.00!
But, when I drove away,
nothing registered
on my gas gauge.
It doesn't show
that I purchased
any gas at all.
I think something
is wrong with that pump.
While I talk to the cashier,
would you mind
checking your gas gauge
to see if you got the gas
you just paid for?"

It seemed like
an odd request,
but I nodded my head "yes"
and headed outside to my car.

I put the key
in the ignition
and anxiously watched
my gas gauge.

Slowly but surely,
the needle moved
away from the "E"
as it made it's way
closer and closer to the "F".

Unlike the gauge
in this young man's truck,
my gauge showed
I had gotten exactly
what I had paid for,
about half a tank of gas.

Looking up from the gauge,
I saw the young man
walking toward my car.

"So, did your gauge move
or is it still sitting
at the same spot
as when you drove in?"

"The pump seems
to be working fine," I answered.
"My gauge is showing
I have about half a tank,
and that's the amount I put in.
Maybe something is wrong
with the gas gauge
in your truck."

"Maybe." he replied.
"Although,
I don't see how
the problem
could be on my end.
I just bought this truck!
It's practically brand new.
I'm pretty sure the problem
is with this pump."

And with that,
disgruntled and upset,
he turned and walked away.

Satisfied with my purchase,
I pulled out of the station
and went on my way.

Later that evening,
as I was reflecting upon
the events of the day,

I thought about the incident
at the gas station.

Both the young man and I
had went to the station
for the same reason.

We had parked
in the same place,
used the same equipment,
talked to the same attendant.

Yet,
only one of us
left there satisfied.

Spiritually,
the same
is often true of us.

Trucking through
the day to day
journey of life,
we look at our
"heart gauge"
and suddenly realize
our hearts are on "E".

Knowing we are in
desperate need
of a fill up,
we head to church,
or read our Bible,
or spend time in prayer.

Some walk away
from this "fill up with God"
full and satisfied,
others are left

Fully Satisfied

feeling empty.

Why?

Like the young man
at the station,
we often fall victim
to a faulty gauge.

Stop and think
about it for a minute.

What do you use
to gauge
Christ's presence
in your own life?

Is it your emotions?

As humans
who are emotionally wired,
this is often
the instrument
we rely on.

Yet probably
nothing is more
unreliable or fickle
than our feelings!

When I entered
the gas station that day,
I had no reason to believe
I would leave there
still on "E".

Why then,
should I believe,
when I enter into

the presence of the living God,
the Creator of the Universe
and the Lover of my soul,
I will walk away
with anything less
than what my heart
needs and desires
the most?

God promises those
who hunger and thirst
for righteousness
will be filled.

Regardless of what
my emotions
may be telling me,
I must believe God
has filled me
to overflowing
with His love,
forgiveness,
wisdom and grace.

I must believe
I have been
strengthened
in my inner man
to once again
run the race
set before me.

I must believe
God is at work
in me and through me.

I must believe
I have received
what I came for!

Fully Satisfied

God is more than able
and more than willing
to dispense His goodness
and His blessings
into our empty hearts.

We simply need
to approach
His throne of grace,
open our heart before Him,
and allow Him to fill us up.

Are you in need of a fill up?
Why not head straight
to the King of Kings
and Lord of Lords?

Believe God
will be faithful
to meet your needs,
then head back
onto the highway of life,
happy and fully satisfied in Him!

Fear Not - 1

God takes us
to many places
in our lives.

Once upon a time,
I had the
awesome privilege
of serving as a nanny.

I was employed
by a wonderful young couple
blessed
with three small boys.

One son attended
a Christian preschool
in the mornings.

One morning
when I arrived
around noon
to pick him up,
I walked in
on a conversation
between his teacher
and one of his fellow classmates.

"Joshua, it's ok, now.
You can take your fingers

38

out of your ears."

Noticing I had
entered the room,
the teacher shared
that the
school fire alarm
had been malfunctioning,
sounding numerous times
over the course
of the morning.

It was obvious
by the look
on Joshua's face,
and of course
the fingers in his ears,
that the alarm
was getting to him.

"Joshua.
Finish coloring
your picture, Honey."

Joshua,
who had no intention
of using his fingers
for anything other
than preventing the
loud, shrill sound
of the alarm
from penetrating
his small ears again,
just sat there.

"Really,
it's ok, Buddy.
I think the men
have fixed the problem.

I don't think
we will hear it
any more today."

"But what if
there's a fire?" he asked.

"Honey,
the fire alarm
isn't going off
because there is
a fire in our school.
It's just not
working right today.

It's ok, though,
because there are
some men here
fixing it.

There is no fire.
Our school is fine. "

"But what if
there IS a fire?"
he asked again.

"Well then,
we will simply do
what we did earlier today
when the alarm went off
and we practiced
our safety drill.
We will go outside
where we will be safe.

It's ok, Joshua.
There is nothing
to worry about.

Finish your picture, Sweetheart."

Still,
Joshua sat
totally immobilized
by the fear
that had gripped
his heart.

"I don't want
to die
in the fire!!!"
he finally screamed.

Walking over
to Joshua
and gently
taking his fingers
out of his ears,
the teacher
knelt down
beside this scared
little three year old
and looked him
right in the eye.

"Don't worry,
Joshua.
I'm right here.
I promise
I won't let
anything
happen to you.

I'll take care of you,
Joshua.
I promise.

Teacher is
right here
with you."

For the first time
since I had
entered the room,
a look of peace
flooded Joshua's face.

It was ok.
He didn't need
to worry.
Teacher was here
and she would
take care of him.
He was safe
because she was
right here with him.

Joshua reached
for his blue crayon.

Soon,
he was back to work
coloring his picture
and sharing in
conversation and laughter
with his classmates.

As I'd witnessed
this scene,
I'd realized
I am a lot
like Joshua.

I have a
tendency
to let the

cares and worries
of this world
grip my heart,
leaving me
paralyzed in fear,
unable to enjoy
all that is going on
around me.

I become
consumed
with fear
and allow it
to steal the life
(not to mention the joy)
right out of me.

As I watched Joshua,
I was reminded
of a acronym
I once heard
for the word fear:

F - false
E - evidence
A - appearing
R - real

This was certainly
the case with Joshua.

Joshua was
fearful
of a fire
that didn't exist.

I, too,
am fearful
of things

that probably
don't exist either,
or most likely
will never even happen.

Yet,
even though
what I fear
is not usually real,
the fear itself
most definitely is!

Maybe you
are like
Joshua and me.

Maybe you also
struggle with fear.

If so,
how can
you and I
learn to
escape fear,
once and for all,
and live
in the freedom
and abundance
of life
Christ wants us
so desperately
to experience?

It's quite simple, really.

Joshua found
his peace
when he
realized

his teacher
was right there
with him
and would take
care of him.

We can partake
of this same
peace
by keeping
our heart and mind
fixed on our
Heavenly Father,
who promises
to never leave us,
nor forsake us.

Even more than
this teacher
could ever hope
to be there
for Joshua,
our God
is there for us.

We don't have
to fear anything
in this life
because our Father
is with us.

I have heard
the phrase
"Fear Not"
is found
365 times
in the Bible.
365 times!

HEARTPRINTS OF GOD – The Early Years

That is
one time
for each day
of the year......
or each day
of our life.

Obviously,
God wants us
to live a life
free of fear.

Fear tries
to take us
prisoner,
causing us
to think
irrationally
and respond
unwisely.

We need
to remember
most fear
comes from Satan.

The Bible tells us
God didn't give us
a spirit of fear,
but rather one
of power,
love
and a sound mind.

Only when
we choose to keep
our focus on Christ,
knowing and believing
He is always with us,

will we be free
from the torment
of fear.

As we rely
on Him
to take
care of us
and to work
all things out
for our good
and His glory,
we will be able
to let go
of fear
and instead
take hold
of the
power,
love
and sound mind
freely available
to us through Christ.

The choice is up to us.

We can either
choose
to sit around
with our fingers
stuck in our ears,
fearful of what
might happen,
all the while
missing out on
what is happening,
or we can
rest in the faithfulness
of our Heavenly Father,

embracing
and thoroughly
enjoying
each and every
minute of our life!

Now.....
where did I
leave my crayon?

Fear Not - 2

God has given each of us
the privilege of being
His hands and feet
to those in need around us.

Just open your eyes
and you will see
opportunity for
giving and sharing
everywhere you look.

I have always been
keenly aware
of these opportunities,
yet shamefully,
I must admit,
I have usually
turned my face
to these calls for help
and avoided them
altogether.

No,
that's not exactly true.

Whenever I've been
given the honor
of helping someone in need
of food, clothing or money,

49

I have always been
more than willing
to share what God
has blessed me with.

This kind of giving is easy.
It's not hard to
drop off a box of food,
or write out a check.

I guess the type of giving
I'm referring to
is the kind that requires
giving of yourself.

For the past six months or so,
my neighbor has been
courageously fighting
a battle with cancer.
I know this not because
I have spoken to her,
but because her husband
has been sharing her struggle
with my husband
during chats over the fence
that separates our yard from theirs.

Knowing she has been facing this,
you would think
I would be doing
whatever I could
to help her, right?

Wrong.

I have instead willfully chosen
to turn my face to her
and her obvious need.

Do I feel guilty about this?
You bet!
Yet, day after day,
I remain silent,
doing absolutely nothing
to help her.

Why?
It's simple.

Fear.

Fear of invading her privacy.
Fear of saying or doing something wrong.
Fear of making her uncomfortable.

Simply put.....
fear of making her situation
worse and not better.

I rationalize
my total complacency
to her need
by convincing myself
she would be
much better off
without me.

And believe it or not......
I actual believe this
to be true.

So, I stay away.

More than ten years ago,
my mother in law
was fighting her own
battle with cancer.
Her eyes

were growing dim
and her strength,
all but gone.

While her family
was in the kitchen
sharing in a meal,
I was sitting at her side.

Feeling so incompetent
to be in this position,
it wasn't a place
I would have chosen to be.

Yet God placed me there
for this moment in time.

As I gazed
upon her frail body,
lying there in her bed,
I noticed her neck,
which appeared to be
in an awkward position.

"Are you OK?" I asked.
"You don't look very comfortable.
Would you like me to try
and adjust your pillow
so you can rest your head
more comfortably?"

With all the energy
she could muster up,
she nodded her head "yes".

Immediately,
fear flooded my entire being.

What am I going to do?
How can I possibly
move her
without hurting her?
If only someone else
was here with me.
I don't know what to do?

With a whirlwind
of thoughts,
doubts and fears
racing through my mind,
I leaned over
this precious woman,
gingerly placing my hand
under her head.

As I tried to
figure out how best
to reposition her
on her pillow,
she reached out
with her own hand,
placing it firmly
on my shoulder.

Then,
using what
little strength she had,
she said
slowly and deliberately,
"DON'T BE AFRAID".

I lifted her head,
readjusted her pillow,
and then gently
laid her head
back down once again.

She looked up at me and smiled.

Those three words,
DON'T BE AFRAID,
were the last words
she spoke to me.

Two days later,
she passed away.

I have carried
those words
in my heart
ever since.

Dying words
meant
to speak life.

Yet, unfortunately,
I have allowed
these words
and the power they bring
to lie dormant
in my heart.

Ten years later,
I am still choosing instead,
to listen
to the lies of Satan.

Lies that only serve
to imprison me
in fear
and render me
totally useless
as God's hands and feet
to those around me.

My neighbor needs me,
and I am not there for her.

And that is my whole point in writing this.

I want to be used by God
no matter how
He chooses to use me.

Be it lending a dollar
or lending my heart.

Until I am willing
to give of myself,
I will never be able
to live up to
the true potential
of my calling
to serve my fellowman.

This giving of myself
will most likely
not be easy
and will most likely
make me
extremely uncomfortable,
but then again....
it's not about me, right?!

It's about forgetting
all about me
so I can instead
focus fully
on the one in need.

It's also about forgetting
my obvious incompetence
and instead,
focusing on the Lord,

who is able.

He is able
to do all
I could ever
think or imagine
and then some!

I know
I am not able
to meet the needs of others,
but the great I AM
certainly is!

All I need to do
is surrender
to my need for Christ
to work in and through me,
and He in turn,
will be faithful
to use me
to meet the needs
He brings before me.

 I love 2 Corinthians 4:7-
*"Now we have
this treasure
in clay jars,
so that this
extraordinary power
may be from God
and not from us."*

No, it's not about easy
and it's not about us.

It's about surrender.
Surrender to all
that is holding me back,

and possibly holding you back, too.

Be it
our pride,
our selfishness,
our laziness
or our fear.

All are simply
tools of Satan
to keep you and I
turning our heads
and walking away.

It's about surrendering
our own meager
talents and abilities
and instead
relying on and trusting in
the limitless power of our God.

It's about surrendering
the urge to turn our face
and walk away,
and instead,
moving forward,
in God-confidence,
to minister
and be used by God.

It's about
making a difference
and making our life
really count!

It's about being
Christ's hands and feet
to a world
so desperately

in need of HIS touch.

I've wasted the last
ten years of my life,
and countless years
before that.
I don't want
to waste
one more second.

It' s about saying
"Here I am, Lord,
use me.
And it's about time
I did.

Let's Talk About It

It was BJ's
first day
at preschool.

He was only two
and this was his
first adventure
away from
the familiarity
and security
of his mother.

As soon as his mother
walked out the door,
leaving BJ behind,
his tears
had started to flow.

And flow they did....
on and on and on,
like a steady river.

I tried everything
I could think of
to bring comfort
to this precious little boy.

I tried showing him
around the room,

pointing out
fun toys and puzzles.
He wasn't interested.

I tried introducing him
to some
of the other children.
He wasn't ready
to make their acquaintance.

I tried reading him a story.
He was only interested
in his own story -
life in a new place,
without his mom.

All throughout the morning,
BJ would cry,
then stop momentarily,
only to stammer,
"I want my mommy"
and then,
start crying
all over again.

*If only I could
get his mind
off his mom
and onto
something else
in this room,*
I thought.

A short while later,
another student,
five year old Benjamin,
walked over to where
we were sitting.

BJ,
still visibly distraught,
had for
the moment
at least,
hushed his crying
and I was hoping
to keep this
tear-free moment
going for the
rest of the day!

"What's wrong with him?"
Benjamin wanted to know.

"Oh, he'll be fine," I said,
"It's his first day,
so everything
is new to him
and he's just feeling
a little uneasy
about being here."

"No," Benjamin replied.
"That's not what's wrong with him.
He misses his mommy."

In a split second,
the word
I had been trying
so desperately
to avoid
was out there.

I was sure
at the mention
of the name, "Mommy",
BJ would once again
burst into tears.

"Uh,
let's not talk
about that,
OK, Benjamin?
I think talking about it
will only make BJ
feel worse.
Let's talk about
something else, OK?"

I now found myself
feeling just as
uncomfortable
as little BJ.

"NO.
I can tell this
is really bothering him
and I think we
should talk about it"
Benjamin said,
as he moved
right up next
to his brand new classmate
and looked him
straight in the eye.

"You miss your mommy,
 don't you?
Well, you know what?
When I first came here,
I missed my Dad.
But don't worry.
My dad always
comes back to get me,
and your mom
will come and get you, too.
Now, dry up those tears.
Wanna play with me?"

To my utter amazement
and total surprise,
BJ wiped his eyes,
climbed off my lap,
then took hold
of Benjamin's hand
as they wondered off to play.

I sat there
totally speechless.

For hours,
I had tried to
bring comfort to BJ,
yet foolishly,
I had totally
missed the mark.

Instead of
tackling the issue
head on,
I had tried
to skirt around it
and avoid it
completely.

Who says
we can't learn
from children?

Benjamin,
having gone through
a similar experience,
was well equipped
to handle this situation.

He knew exactly
what BJ was feeling,
and spoke to the heart

of what was
bothering little BJ
the most -
fear of abandonment.

Once Benjamin
reassured BJ
his mother would
eventually
come back
for him,
he was free
to play and have fun.

How many times
have you and I
skirted around issues,
not wanting
to bring any more
pain or discomfort
to those around us?

We casually talk
about the weather,
share in politics,
or talk about
the cost of groceries,
all the while
missing the mark totally.

Sometimes,
the best thing
we can do
is to talk about it.

Yes,
it might be
awkward at first.
And yes,

it may stir up
painful memories
or buried hurts,
but in the end,
it will bring
comfort and healing.

There is
something powerful
in talking to someone
who has been there
and experienced first hand
what we our self
are going through.

There is also something
equally powerful
about sharing
your own experience
and your testimony
with someone
who is now
walking down a road
you have already traveled.

I am a firm believer
that pain has a purpose.

We will all suffer pain
in some form or another
in our lifetime.

The choice, then,
is not will we hurt,
but rather
what will we do
with our hurt.

We can choose
to allow the hurt
to take root
in our heart,
producing
loneliness,
bitterness
or apathy,
or we can
choose to find
the purpose in our pain,
and instead
use our own experience
to help someone else.

Then, and only then,
will our pain
begin to reveal
its purpose.

Purpose, in turn,
will bring with it
strength,
restoration
and healing.

The Bible tells us
to comfort one another
with the comfort
we have been given.

The only way
we can do this
is to talk about it -
openly and honestly.

Is there some hurt
in your life
that you have been

carrying around
way too long?

Why not find
someone whom you trust,
and talk about it?

Is there someone
you know
who could use
a listening ear
and an understanding heart?

Why not ask
the Holy Spirit
to give you
the words they need,
and then approach that person.

Let's quit ignoring
the issues of our hearts.

Why should we choose
to settle for only pain,
when God
has so much more
in store for us,
if we are simply willing
to talk about it.

My Hope is is Thee

As I hung up the phone,
I could hardly breathe.

The news was simply
too wonderful to contain.
I felt as though my heart
would burst with
joy and excitement.

My husband and I
were going to have a baby...
a dream come true.

This wasn't the first time
I had heard these words
from the doctor
or experienced this
overwhelming flood of emotion.

Twice before,
I had been able
to surprise my husband
with this same,
wonderful news
and watch
as his face lit up,
and his eyes sparkled.

My Hope is is Thee

We both have
a deep love for children
and having one of our own
was a dream
we both shared
and talked about often.

Twice before, however,
I had also known
the deep sorrow
and silent grief
that rips your heart apart
when you lose
that little life
before you have ever
had a chance
to meet
your son or daughter
face to face,
or embrace
and tenderly kiss them.

This time was going
to be different, though.
I just knew it.
I could feel hope
running
all throughout my body,
from my head to my toes!

I had lost my father
eight months earlier,
and I felt as though this
was God's way
of bringing new life
back into mine
and joy
back into my heart.

I could hardly wait
to tell my husband
and the rest of the world.

Even though
my faith was strong,
and my hope sure,
I have to admit,
there were moments
when I would start
to worry about losing
this precious little one, too.

When those moments came,
however,
God was always faithful
to send a reminder
to keep me hoping.

Like the time
I was sitting
in a hospital waiting room,
waiting to have some
routine blood work done.

I started to feel anxious,
but before I had a chance
to dwell on these feelings,
a beautiful little girl,
about three years old,
came and sat down
right next to me.

We talked and laughed
and had the best time.

After a few minutes,
I asked her
what her name was.

My Hope is is Thee

"Esperanza" she replied.

"What a beautiful name.
Your name means
hope in English,
doesn't it?" I asked.

She just smiled,
but her mother nodded
and said, "Yes, it does."

Instantly,
my fear vanished
and hope ruled my heart.
God was with me
and everything
was going to be just fine.

Weeks flew by and soon,
at my six weeks Dr. visit,
I was able to not only
see my baby,
but to hear
the beating of its heart.

"Your baby has
a very strong heartbeat.
Everything looks
and sounds terrific!"
the doctor declared.

Still, as days went on,
fear tried desperately
to steal my joy.

With each moment of fear,
however,
God was faithful
to send me

a hope-filled moment
to hold on to.

Like the time
I was driving home
from work
and caught myself
once again fearful
of facing yet another miscarriage
and another heartbreak.

Turning a corner,
a sign at a church
beckoned for my attention.
There,
for all the world to see,
were God's words of hope.

Now may the God
of hope
fill you with
all joy and peace
as you believe
so that you may
overflow with hope
by the power
of the Holy Spirit.
~Romans 15:13

I pulled over
to the side of the road,
found a pen and paper,
and copied down
this powerful word
from God.

I decided,
right then and there,
to commit this

particular scripture
to memory.
The next time Satan
tried to bring
doubt or fear
to my heart or mind,
I would hold up
my shield of faith
and quench his fiery dart
by boldly proclaiming
the hope in my heart.

Weeks turned into months...
three to be exact.

Then,
my hope died,
right along
with the death
of the tiny life
I had carried inside me.

I was devastated.
This time was suppose
to be different.

How could this
be happening again,
especially after God
had been so deliberate
in His attempts
to encourage me
to keep hoping,
to keep believing?

I felt totally and completely numb.

To be totally honest,
I felt as though God

73

had been teasing me.

He knows the end
from the beginning.
He knew this pregnancy
was going to end
just like the two before it,
and yet He kept
dangling hope
out there in front of me.

My numbness
soon turned to
anger and bitterness.

Time went by
and I struggled
to keep my relationship
with the Lord
vibrant and strong.

I had walked
with the Lord
long enough to know
His true character:
all love, all mercy,
all wisdom, all the time.

I knew God loved me
and wanted only
the best for me.

I knew He was always
working all things
for my good and His glory.

I knew what Satan
meant for harm,
He could and would

use for my good.

My head knew
all of this,
but my heart,
oh my heart.
It felt betrayed.
It had dared to hope.

Then one night,
as I was reading
in the Psalms,
God,
in his tenderness,
revealed to me
the true substance
of the hope
He kept placing
in my heart
during those three months.

I suddenly realized
that my hope
had been completely
misplaced.

All that time,
I had been
placing my hope
in the life I carried,
not in the ONE
who was carrying me.

God did know
how this pregnancy
would end.
He knew my heart
would once again
be broken

into a million pieces.
He knew all of this
and because He did,
He was preparing me
for this loss
by placing seeds of hope
into my heart.

Not hope in my baby,
but hope in HIM!

Tears filled my eyes,
once again,
as I found myself
on my knees
thanking God
for being
all loving, all merciful,
all wise, all the time.

Over and over again
in the Bible,
we find
verse after verse
leading us
to the only one
we can truly
place our hope in.

Be strong,
and let your heart
be courageous,
all you who
put your
hope in the LORD.
~Psalm 31:24

Now, Lord,
what do I wait for?

My hope is in you.
~Psalm 39:7

Happy is the one
whose help is the
God of Jacob,
whose **hope is in
the LORD his God.**
~Psalm 146:5

Blessed is the man
that trusts in the LORD,
And whose
hope is the LORD.
~Jeremiah 17:7 NJKV

Now,
years later,
I would love
to be able
to tell you
my heart
no longer feels
the pain
of these losses,
but that wouldn't
be true.

Not a day goes by
that I don't
feel the hurt.

Yet,
through the hurt,
I have chosen
to keep placing
my hope
in my God.

As I allow
the God of hope
to fill me
with joy and peace
in believing,
I abound with hope,
through the power
of the Holy Spirit.

Have you ever
been disappointed
by God?

Have you ever
felt as though
He dangled hope
in front of you
only to lead you
to heartache?

If so,
I encourage you
to take a closer look.

Could it be,
like me,
your hope
was misplaced?

The world
and all that is in it
will let us down,
abandon us,
and leave us
broken hearted,
but our God
who is all love,
all mercy,
all wise,

all the time,
never will.

Put your hope
in Him
and I guarantee,
you won't be disappointed.

The Real Deal

My grandma,
born and raised
in the deep South,
was a spunky lady,
to say the least.

She had a dry,
witty sense of humor
and was famous
for her one-liners.

While her words
always brought a laugh,
they also revealed
her wisdom.

Long after
the laughter faded,
her words resonated
in my heart.

As a young, single woman
in my early twenties,
I often traveled by myself.

I thought nothing
of getting in my car
and driving
seven hours north

to see my parents,
or ten hours east
to spend time
with my sister.

My parents, however,
worried about my safety.

Time after time,
they cautioned me
of the dangers
of traveling alone.

One time,
this familiar
topic of conversation
came up
while we were
visiting my grandma.

"I don't know why
she insists
on traveling by herself,"
my mother said,
as I sat
right beside her
on my Grandma's turquoise couch.

"I keep telling her
to get a man's hat
and place it
in her back window.
That way,
it would at least
look like a man
was traveling with her.
For all they know,
he could simply
be taking a nap

in the backseat!"

Without skipping a beat,
my Grandma
leaned forward,
looked directly at me
and remarked,
"Forget about the hat, honey.
Get a man!"

Laughter spilled into the room.

Then Grandma continued.

"Who wants
a silly ole hat
when you can have
the real deal?!"

And of course,
for all practical purposes,
Grandma was right!

I understood
my mother's reasoning
and felt her love for me
in this odd request,
but I had to agree
with my Grandma.

What good
would a hat do?
It was,
after all,
just a hat.

At a quick glance,
it might
give the appearance

The Real Deal

that a man
was along for the ride,
but appearances and reality
are two totally different things!

Could a hat
change
a flat tire
for me?

Could a hat
take the wheel
and drive for me
if I got tired
and needed a break
from the driver's seat?

Could a hat
protect me
from a would be assailant?

No,
the hat was
merely for show
and would only provide
a false
sense of security.

I didn't need a hat,
I needed a man!

As ridiculous
as I found
my mother's idea
to be,
I couldn't deny
the joke was on me
when it came
to my spiritual life.

I had grown up
in a Christian home
and had attended church
from a young age.

I knew all
about God,
the Bible,
and what it meant
to look
like a Christian.

In fact,
anyone driving
by my life
would have been sure
to notice
my Bible,
my Christian lingo
and my Christian ways.

But,
if they would have
gotten close enough
to peer into
the backseat of my heart,
they would have discovered
all these
were just for show.

I was traveling life alone.

I had religion,
but what I needed
was the man,
Christ Jesus.

It wasn't until
my earlier thirties

that I traded in
my religious facade
for a true,
vibrant,
living and breathing
relationship with the Lord.

Through the power
of the Holy Spirit,
God became real to me
for the first time
in my life.

Now,
my Bible
is no longer
on display
for all to see,
but instead,
its words
are hidden in my heart,
guiding,
leading
and transforming me
little by little,
day by day.

The words I speak
are no longer spoken
to impress others
with my spirituality,
but rather
to impress upon others
the beauty and freedom
that can be found
in a relationship
with Christ.

I pray each day
God will
take the wheel
of my life
and live
in and through me.

I am no longer
satisfied
with a religion
that is just
for show,
and why should I be?

Think about it.

Can religion
forgive my sins?

Can religion
create
a new heart
in me?

Can religion
live in
and through me?

Can religion
feel my hurt,
understand my fears,
or speak to my heart?

No, only Christ can.

Why would I want
to settle for
anything less
than the real deal?

The Real Deal

And, why should you?

Oh, by the way,
in case
you are wondering,
I took my
Grandma's advice
and got a man.

I not only have
Christ in my life,
but a
wonderful husband, too!

No more
traveling alone
for this girl!

From now on,
it's the three of us
sharing every
single moment
of this amazing ride
called life!

The Wisdom of a Father

Several years ago,
when my father's
health was declining,
my mother found herself
carrying the heavy load
of caregiver
along with her other
daily responsibilities.

Eventually,
it became apparent
to all in our family,
that she was in need
of a time of respite.

My mother asked
my sister and I
to return home,
care for our father,
and give her
some much needed
time away.

We agreed
and hesitantly,
she packed her bags
and headed
for the home
of my father's sister.

The Wisdom of a Father

Each evening,
my mother would call
to check on my father
and to see
how things were
in her absence.

The first few phone calls
confirmed that we
had made the right decision
in "sending" her away.
Her voice still
sounded tired
and she mentioned
she was sleeping a lot.

Several days into her trip,
however,
after some much needed
rest and relaxation,
her phone conversations
became more lively,
full of laughter and excitement.

My aunt,
her hostess,
was going out of her way
to make sure
my mom was waited on
hand and foot
and my mom
seemed to be
thoroughly enjoying
this arrangement.

Each day she
would tell of the
delicious food they ate,
the wonderful places they visited,

and the lavish attention
my aunt was giving her.

One night
after speaking with my mom,
and hearing all about her day,
my dad asked to speak
to his sister,
the gracious hostess.

What he told her
made us all laugh.

"Don't be spoiling her
too much now.
I'm the one who
has to live with her,
you know!"

Of course,
he was teasing,
but the thought
behind the laugh
opened my mind
to a spiritual truth.

Too much of a good thing
can become a bad thing.

More than my aunt
wanted to bless
my mother,
God longs
to bless us.
He delights in
showering His children
with blessings.

The Wisdom of a Father

Yet,
even something
as beautiful as
a heavenly blessing,
when given to
a heart that fails
to recognize or appreciate it,
can begin to have
a very repulsive
human stench.

We have all
smelled it and
it isn't pretty.

No wonder we
refer to someone
in this condition
as "spoiled".

Often,
when God's blessings
runneth over
and we find our self
in need of nought,
we become untouched
by the generosity
of our Heavenly Father.

Blessings pour
into our life
and we barely take notice,
much less
offer words of thanksgiving
to the Giver
of all good gifts.

Other times,
however,

the problem is
not that we
don't notice the blessings.

Quite the opposite.

Oddly enough,
when we have
received so bountifully
from the hand of God
we can come
to a place in our
relationship with the Lord
where we begin
to *expect* such blessings,
then become bitter
when they don't
rain down on us
as we feel they should.

We become spoiled
by the selfless love
of our gracious God
and our actions
and attitude
attest to it!

Yes,
God loves to
lavish gifts
upon his children,
but like my father,
He is very wise.

He understands
what we don't.

The rest of the world
has to live with us!

Two Words That Change Everything

One night while I was
getting ready for bed,
I tuned in to my favorite
Christian radio station.

A woman was sharing
a story of God's faithfulness.
I listened as she told
of God's miraculous intervention
in her life during a time
when all looked hopeless.

As she recounted God's goodness
and told of the supernatural way
He had worked in behalf
of her and her children,
she very casually spoke two words.

Two small words,
and yet this phrase
completely captured my attention,
transforming my thinking
and ultimately, my faith in God.

I don't know how her story ended.
As I tried to grasp the implications
of these two words,

my mind became
totally consumed
with this new knowledge
God was imparting to me
through her testimony.

I kept repeating the phrase
over and over,
out loud,
and each time the words
penetrated my ears,
the truth behind them
penetrated my heart.

I suddenly found myself
strengthened in my
inner most being.

I literally felt
the touch of God
on my heart.

I knew,
at that very moment,
my relationship
with the Lord
had entered a
deeper,
more intimate,
faith-filled level.

How could two small words
make such a
radical difference
in my life?

Simple.

These two words

Two Words That Change Everything

change everything!
Most likely,
they will change you, too!

But God.

But God.

Say it aloud
and let the truth
and reality of these words
penetrate your own heart.

But God.

No matter what is
going on in your life,
or what you may
be going through,
know and remember
all things must surrender
to the power
and authority
of our God.

Right now,
at this very moment,
stop and think about
what you are
struggling with today.

Whatever it may be,
I guarantee it is
no match for our God.

The Bible is living proof of that!

The Israelites had
Pharaoh's army

breathing down their neck
and the Red Sea
in front of them,

BUT GOD.....

David had only
a little bitty sling shot
with which to slay
a giant of a man
named Goliath,

BUT GOD...

Daniel was served
as the main course
to a den of lions
known for their
ferocious appetites,

BUT GOD...

A widow was
out of time and
out of money,
with only a houseful
of empty containers
she had collected
from her neighbors,

BUT GOD...

Jonah was sinking
in his sin of rebellion
and headed for the
bottom of the ocean,

BUT GOD...

Two Words That Change Everything

Jesus was
crucified,
dead,
and buried,

BUT GOD...

Time and time again,
when all looked hopeless
and those in the
midst of the situation
felt most helpless,
God showed up and did
the seemingly impossible.

Does your situation appear hopeless?
Are you feeling helpless?

Take heart.

God is the same yesterday, today and forever.

Instead of ending
the circumstances
of your life
with a period,
replace the finality
of your thinking
with a comma
of hope,
followed by your
declaration of faith!

Boldly look
your situation
in the face
and speak
the only two words
that are able
to breathe life

into your faith
and power
into your life.

I am (fill in the blank), BUT GOD...

I don't see how I can (fill in the blank), BUT GOD...

I don't have (fill in the blank), BUT GOD...

I am scared that (fill in the blank), BUT GOD...

So, what are you waiting for?

Go ahead!
Let God write
the ending
of your story.

If you do,
I have no doubt
He will finish
all things
that pertain to you
with a true
exclamation
of His glory
and His marvelous grace!

True Refreshment

A few months ago,
after a long day at work,
I couldn't wait to get home,
trade my shoes
for a pair of flip flops,
and step out into
the shade and relaxation
waiting for me
on our back patio.

Each afternoon,
I would unwind
from work
by sitting outside,
sipping on a cool drink
and taking in
the beauty of our yard.

Imagine my surprise,
when I drew back the blinds
and reached for the handle
of our sliding glass door,
only to find
sunlight flooding
not only our backyard,
but every single inch
of our patio.

How could this be?

What had happened
to our shady backyard?

Evidently,
while I had been
slaving away at work,
someone else
had been slaving away
pruning the trees
in the yard
that backs up
to ours.

The huge cottonwood
that had once
provided shade
for both our yard
and our patio,
now barely
made any shade at all.

The heat
from the sun
was intense
and so was
my disappointment.

While the tree
was most certainly
in need of a "haircut",
I questioned the timing.

Now?!
In the middle of July?

Now?!
When shade was in hot demand?

True Refreshment

Now?!
When each afternoon,
I counted on
the long branches
of this tree
to provide me
with a cool oasis
in the midst of
the southwestern desert heat!

NO!
This was all wrong.

How could this tree
let me down like this?
I needed it to
stand up tall
and be a tree!
I needed some shade
to kick back
and relax in!

As I stood there
looking out my
sliding glass door,
covered from
head to toe
by the sunlight
now streaming in,
God used this moment
to illuminate my own life
and speak to my heart.

Everywhere we look
and every place we go,
we find people in need
of a spiritual oasis.

The struggles,
trials,
and heartaches
that often accompany life
can be relentless at times,
beating down on us
until we are weak,
dehydrated and
desperately in need
of a time of refreshment.

God created
you and me
to be an umbrella
of His love
to those in need.

Our prayers,
our words of encouragement,
our helping hands
or listening ears
can help to shield
a hurting heart
from the heat of life.

Just like I counted
on the cottonwood tree
to be there for me,
people in our lives
are counting on us.

How many times
have I
disappointed others
by failing
to provide them
with the "shade"
they are so desperately
counting on?

True Refreshment

How many times
have I
taken care
of my own needs
without giving any thought
to the timing
or the subsequent
consequences
of my actions
in the lives
of those around me?

How many people
have come to me
hoping to find
shelter from the
heat of the battles
in their lives
only to be
disappointed with my
lack of interest,
lack of compassion
and lack of support?

As I slowly
closed the blinds,
I realized God
was doing some
pruning of His own...
in my heart.

Maybe God
was calling me
to stand up
and be the
child of God
He had created
me to be.

Maybe,
instead of
going out into
my backyard,
God was challenging me
to step out
my front door
and into the lives
of those around me.

Maybe God
was desperately trying
to open my heart
to the simple truth
found in Proverbs 11:25, NLT:
"those who refresh others
will themselves be refreshed"

Maybe,
my finding shade
wasn't nearly as important
as my giving it away to others.

The Gift of Today

"Stacy, I need you
  to fast forward this part."

The request came
from a four year old.
He and his older brother
were watching a movie
we had checked out
from our local library
earlier that morning.

Even though both boys
had seen this movie
several times before,
it had still made its way
into our book bag
and now,
into their DVD player.

"Why, honey?" I asked.
"Is this part upsetting to you?"

"No.
I just don't want
to watch this part.
It's boring.
I want to hurry up
and look at the funny part."

"Well, you can't hurry up!"
His six year old brother
now jumped into
our conversation.
"You have to
go through the part
you don't like
so you can get
to the funny part.
It's all part of the movie
and that's just the way it is."

I never cease
to be amazed
at the simple,
yet profound words
of wisdom
commonly spoken
by children.

Countless times,
my heart
has been pricked
and my thoughts sparked
by their keen observations
and raw honesty.

"Ohhhh kaaaaaaaaaaay,"
the younger brother replied.
"I'll look at the TV,
but I'm not really
going to watch it!"

And so it is with life.

How many times
have you and I
wished we could simply
hit the fast forward button

and speed through
a time in our life
that wasn't exactly
pleasing to us?

How many times
have you and I
looked at life,
but not really lived it?

If the truth be told,
most of us,
whether we
realize it or not,
are inevitably
living our life
in fast forward.

"What?" You say.
"Not me."

I hate to burst your bubble,
but does T.G.I.F. ring a bell?
Thank God it's Friday?
I thought so.

If you are like me,
there have probably been
numerous times
in your own life
when you have
climbed out of bed
Monday morning
already thinking about
the upcoming weekend.

If I can just make it
through the week,
then I can enjoy

the weekend.

Sadly, five whole days –
Monday,
Tuesday,
Wednesday,
Thursday,
and Friday –
are passed over
in an effort
to hurry through
the part we don't like
in hopes of getting
to the part we do.

Before we know it,
our entire life
has passed before us
or worse yet,
passed us by.

Every single day
is a unique
and precious gift
from God.

Just like a snowflake
or the prints on your thumb,
no two days are alike.

We only get
one chance
to live this day.

In the light
of that great revelation,
isn't it absolutely bizarre
that we don't choose
to be more selective

and more intentional
about the way we spend
each moment
God has so graciously
given to us?

Sure,
we both have obligations,
such as work
and family responsibilities,
that may dictate
to some degree
how our twenty-four hours
of time are spent,
but ultimately,
you and I
are the only ones
in control
of our day.

It is you and I
who have been
given
the final say
as to whether
we will spend
this never-to-be-lived-again
moment of time
happy or miserable,
thankful or complaining,
giving or taking,
doing or watching,
enjoying or enduring,
living or going through the motions.

The choice is ours
and ours alone.

"But wait," you say.
"That's not true.
You don't know
how demanding
and difficult
my boss can be.
You don't know
the pressure
I'm under financially.
You don't know
about my illness.
You haven't seen
my to-do list.
You just don't know
what I am going through."

You're right.
I don't.

But I do know this.

When the sun
sets this evening,
our today will vanish
only to become
yet another one
of our yesterdays.

It will be over,
never to be lived
again.

Life passes
all too quickly.
Each day begins
and ends
before we have
barely had time
to make its acquaintance.

The Gift of Today

Shouldn't we choose
to live
every single moment
of today,
regardless of whether
the moment is
good or bad,
happy or sad?

Why should we
long to hit
the fast forward button,
when one day
we will inevitably
long to press rewind
and live moments
of our life
all over again?

Time is ticking.
Let's start making
the most
of this precious gift
and truly start living!

*This is the day
the Lord has made;
let's rejoice
and be glad in it.*
~Psalm 118:24

Loving in His Name

After graduating
from college,
the Lord led me
to New Jersey
and to what would
turn out to be
one of the most
rewarding experiences
of my life.

My college roommate
and dear friend
had accepted
a teaching position
at a Christian school there
and told me about
an opening
at a daycare center
located next door
to her school.

Having never ventured
east of the Mississippi,
this new opportunity
sounded inviting.

After much prayer,
I packed my bags
and headed

Loving in His Name

for the East coast.

To my delight,
I was assigned
a class of
adorable,
rambunctious,
lovable
two and three year olds.

Each day
was an adventure
in learning...
them from me,
and most often,
me from them.

I taught these
free-spirited little ones
how to be still
and stand
in a straight line.

They taught me
to walk
to the beat
of my own drum.

I taught these
creative minds
how to
hold a paintbrush
and a crayon.
They taught me
how to
hold my head high
and be proud
of who I am.

I taught these children
who were destined
for greatness,
how to write their name.
Four years later,
Stephanie would teach me
it's not your name
that's important;
it's the love
you give away.

Stephanie was
a beautiful,
energetic
three year old.

Every day
she came dressed
in the cutest outfits
accompanied
by a smile
that would light up the room.

At a casual glance,
one would have assumed
Stephanie's life
was as beautiful
as she was.

Sadly,
this notion
was far
from the reality
of her situation.

Both her
mother and father
were in prison
and she was living

with her grandparents.

Even though her
living arrangement
had changed
for the better,
deep inside,
Stephanie still lived
with the hurt,
pain and abuse
that had been
such a part
of the first three years
of her young life.

All of my students
quickly
warmed up to me
and welcomed me
into their world.

All,
that is,
except Stephanie.

She kept
her guard up
and never let herself
get too close
or too comfortable
with anyone.

How my heart
broke for her.

Each day
I prayed the Lord
would pour out
His perfect love

through me,
freeing Stephanie
from her own prison
of hurt,
pain
and loneliness;
healing this
precious little girl
of her brokenness.

Weeks turned into months.

As we spent time
together each day,
Stephanie gradually
began to lower
the emotional wall
that had separated
her from me.

One memorable day,
as we were
taking a walk
in a nearby park,
I felt a little hand
take hold of mine.

It was Stephanie's.

From that moment on,
Stephanie and I
were heart to heart.

The year soon
came to an end
and so did my time
with these precious children.

Loving in His Name

I had accepted
a teaching position
in Wisconsin
and was headed
to the Mid-west.

Four years later,
my husband and I
had the opportunity
to visit my friend
in New Jersey
and to once again
go to the daycare
where I had taught.

As I experienced
the familiarity
of each classroom
and gazed into the eyes
of the children
now attending,
I couldn't help wishing
I could once again
see the children
who had touched
my heart
four years earlier.

I casually shared
this desire
with one
of the current teachers.

Naturally,
the children
in my class
had long since
moved on
to other

cities and schools.

One child,
however,
had enrolled
at the Christian school
next door.

Imagine
the joy
I felt
when I learned
this child
was none other
than Stephanie.

We excitedly
made our way
to the school
and then
to Stephanie's classroom.

I anxiously
peeked
through the window
in the classroom door
and began
scouring
the sea of children
for this one
familiar face.

From the
far corner
of the room,
a young girl
turned around
to speak
to a fellow classmate.

Loving in His Name

As she did,
she spotted me
peering through
the window
and immediately
came running
in my direction.

I burst
into the room
and ran to meet her.

Stephanie buried
her head
in my stomach
as she embraced me
with every ounce
of her being.

When she finally
lifted her head
and turned
her beautiful face
upward
to look at me,
I couldn't believe
God had blessed me
with this unexpected reunion.

As I looked
into her eyes,
I asked
in total amazement,
"You still
remember me
after all these years?
You were just
three years old
when I last saw you."

Then Stephanie
said the words
I will never forget;
words that brought tears
not only to my eyes,
but also to the eyes
of my husband
as he witnessed
one of the most
priceless moments
of my entire life.

"I don't remember your name,"
she said,
"but I know you love me".

How fitting
that Stephanie
didn't remember my name.

My name wasn't important.

Who I was didn't matter.

Amazingly,
I was
simply the one,
handpicked by God,
to touch the heart
of this precious child
with His healing love.

What an awesome honor
I had been given.

My name
had long since
been forgotten,
but it was

Loving in His Name

obvious
the love
she had received
never would be.

As I stood
captivated
in this divinely orchestrated
moment in time,
I humbly thanked God.

I thanked Him
for leading me
to New Jersey.

I thanked Him
for bringing Stephanie
into my classroom
and into my life.

I thanked Him
for His incredible love
that sets
the captives free
and heals
the most broken
of hearts.

I thanked him
for the incredible
honor
we have all
been given:
to love others in HIS name.

Crouching At the Door

One of the perks
of having a husband
is having
your very own
small game hunter.

At least that's the way
I like to refer
to the man of my house.

Anytime an
eight legged creature
or otherwise
unwelcome guest
is spotted,
my husband
is beckoned
and voila!

Bug be gone!

It's like having
my very own
personal exterminator.

The only problem is
my man isn't always home
when one of these
small beasts

decides
to pay us a visit.

Such was the case
one night
several weeks ago.

With my husband
out of the house
for a few hours,
I decided
to take advantage
of my time alone
to do some household chores,
one of which was laundry.

With a basketful of clothes
tucked under my arm,
I made my way
to our garage
where our
washer and dryer
are located.

After I started the load,
I headed back
toward the door
leading from the garage
into our home.

As I reached
for the doorknob,
I just happened
to look up,
spotting
on the ceiling
a scorpion
who just happened to be
looking down at me.

As our eyes met,
I knew there
was only one thing
to do.
I darted
into the house
as fast as I could,
quickly closing the door
behind me.

Then,
I calmly
and casually
strolled
into the living room
acting as though
this brief encounter
had never happened.

Try as I may,
though,
I couldn't erase
the image
of the scorpion
from my mind.

I knew it was out there.

I had seen it
and all the pretending
in the world
wasn't going
to change that.

I also knew
this fella
had legs.

Crouching At the Door

It wasn't going
to be content
to simply hang out
on the ceiling
of our garage.

Before long,
it would decide
to venture indoors.

Like it or not,
I knew
I had to kill it
before it had a chance
to crawl under the door
and make itself at home
in *our* home.

Mustering up
all the courage
I could find,
I headed back
out to the garage.

I picked up
my husband's
weapon of choice,
a long stick,
and proceeded
to do some
small game hunting
of my own.

After numerous shrieks
(from me, not the scorpion),
this would be
home invader soon
fell lifeless
to the floor.

Mission accomplished.

As I made my way
through the doorway
and back into our home,
I was reminded
of the words
found in Genesis 4:7,
*"sin is crouching
at the door".*

Remember the story?

God had asked
for an animal sacrifice,
but Cain,
being a tiller
of the ground,
had instead
offered the Lord
a sacrifice
of fruits and vegetables.

When God
didn't accept
Cain's offering,
Cain became angry.

God knew
if Cain did not
squelch this anger
before it had time
to consume his heart,
sin would soon follow.

Foolishly,
Cain walked away
from God's counsel.

It didn't take long
for his anger
to take over
his thoughts
and subsequently,
his actions.

In the very next verse,
in fact,
we read the sad details.

Cain lured his brother,
Abel,
out into a field
and killed him.

All too often,
instead of
eradicating the sin
in our life
once and for all,
we foolishly
allow it to remain
at the threshold.

Sometimes,
we pretend
it doesn't exist.

We go on
about our life
as though
there is nothing
to be concerned about.

Oftentimes,
however,
we do acknowledge it,
but in our arrogance,

we proudly
parade around it
as though
we are invincible
and the sin incapable
of penetrating
the walls of our heart.

Like Cain,
when we willfully
allow sin
to take root
in our heart,
the following verses
of our own life
will eventually reveal
the sad details.

Sin comes
packaged
with consequences.

As the sin
plays itself out
in our life,
we too may discover
our actions
have "killed" something
very dear
to our own heart.

Maybe it is
our reputation
that received
the deadly blow.

Perhaps it is
our marriage
that is now

lifeless and dead.

Possibly,
it may even be
our very will
to live
that is found
gasping
for its next breath.

The scorpion
in my garage
didn't stand a chance.

Unfortunately,
neither do
you and I
when it comes
to sin.

In our own power,
we are completely
incapable
of battling
this invader
of our heart.

How we need a savior.

Have you checked
the doorway
of your heart
lately?

Is there a sin
lying in wait
for an opportune time
to make its way
into your life?

If so,
don't wait
another minute.

Call upon your Heavenly Father.

When we
confess our sins
to God,
He is ever faithful
to come to our rescue.

His weapon of choice
has always been
the blood he shed
for you and me
on the cross of Calvary.

As we confess
and then repent,
God covers this sin
with His precious blood,
giving us
the ultimate victory.

With hands held high
in praise and thanksgiving
to our God,
we can once and for all
boldly declare,
"Mission accomplished!"

His True Destiny Was to Change Ours

Several years ago
while shopping
an after-Christmas sale,
I stumbled onto
a priceless treasure.

I was digging through
a huge bin
of marked down T-shirts
when I saw
a navy blue one
peeking out
from near the bottom
of the pile.

Since blue
has always been
my color of choice,
I decided this shirt
was worth going after.

After several minutes
of elbowing my way
through a sea of shirts,
the one that caught my eye
was finally within my reach.

As I picked it up,
I turned it over
and looked at the front.

To my surprise,
the design
on this T-shirt
was that
of the manger scene.

Little baby Jesus
was fast asleep
in his small cradle,
with Mary tenderly seated
as his side.

As beautiful as this was,
more beautiful yet,
were the six words
printed boldly in white
above the picture.

His Destiny Was to Change Ours

Here was the true
meaning of Christmas
spelled out
for all to see
and yet
up until now,
this T-shirt
had slipped by
totally unnoticed
and completely unseen,
buried at the bottom
of a clearance bin!

As I stood there,
surrounded

His True Destiny Was to Change Ours

by a crowd of
noisy, energetic shoppers,
I felt a hush
come over my soul.

Day in
and day out
we elbow
our way through life
in an effort to
reach our goals,
get ahead,
succeed,
and find true happiness.

Digging through
the bin of life,
we proudly grab
these surface level bargains,
settling for the leftovers
of this world,
all the while
missing out
on our true destiny.

We go to church
and accept
the surface level truth
of Christ's birth,
yet never realize
the very essence of Christ
and the purpose
of his arrival
as a tiny baby
may still remain buried
under piles of ill-fitting
religion and theology.

How we need
to dig deeper,
to search more,
to grasp
the almost incomprehensible......
His destiny *was* to *change* ours!

Yes,
Christ came to earth
as a baby
to ultimately
die on the cross,
making a way of
forgiveness,
atonement and
salvation for us.
There is no denying
this life-giving truth.

Our final
and ultimate destiny
is to be with Him
in Heaven
throughout all eternity.

But what about here?

What about now?

One of my favorite verses
is John 10:10.
If ever a verse
described
the destiny of Jesus
as it relates to ours,
this is it.

*"I have come
so that they*

His True Destiny Was to Change Ours

may have life
and have it
in abundance."

Life eternal
is most definitely
part of the abundance part,
but our destiny
doesn't begin
once our time
on this earth is over.

NO!

Our destiny changes
the moment we
turn our life
over to Christ.

Our can'ts become cans.

For I can do everything
through Christ
who gives me strength.
~Philippians 4:13, NLT

Our defeats become victories.

No, in all these things
we are more than conquerors
through him who loved us.
~Romans 8:37

Our trials become treasures.

We know that all things
work together for the good
of those who love God,
who are called according

to his purpose.
~Romans 8:28

Our desires become reality.

Take delight in the Lord,
and he will give you
your heart's desires.
~Psalms 37:4

I'm so glad
I caught
a glimpse of blue
peeking out
from the bottom
of that bin
of marked down T-shirts.

Yet no happiness
in the world
will ever begin
to match the joy
I now feel
since I caught
a glimpse
of my true destiny
in Christ.

When it comes
to shopping,
you will still find me
searching through
clearance bins
in hopes
of finding a bargain.

But thanks be to God,
you will
never, ever

His True Destiny Was to Change Ours

find me digging
through the
bargain bins of life
or poking through
the discounted racks
of religion and theology.

I have discovered
my true destiny
and I'm not settling
for anything less
than God's best for me!

I am not going
to wait until I die
to truly start to live.

I am going to live
the abundant life now!

I am going
to reach out
with every bit
of my
heart,
mind
and soul
and grab onto
the treasure
I have in Christ.

I am going
to start living out
my Christ-given destiny.

How about you?

You will seek me
and find me
when you
search for me
with all of your heart.
~Jeremiah 29:13

Answering His Call

One morning
as I came before the Lord,
opening His Word,
He led me to
Jeremiah 1:4-10, NLT

The LORD gave me
this message:

"I knew you before
I formed you
in your mother's womb.
Before you were born
I set you apart
and appointed you
as my prophet to the nations."

"O Sovereign LORD," I said,
"I can't speak for you!
I'm too young!"

The LORD replied,
"Don't say, 'I'm too young,'
for you must go
wherever I send you
and say whatever I tell you.
And don't be afraid
of the people,
for I will be with you

and will protect you.
I, the LORD, have spoken!"

Then the LORD
reached out
and touched my mouth
and said,
"Look,
I have put my words
in your mouth!"
~Jeremiah 1:4-10a, NLT

I smiled
as I read
the words of Jeremiah.
I wonder
if God smiled, too.

After all,
this wasn't
the first time
the Lord had heard
this kind of response
after issuing
a call of duty.

Remember Moses?
He expressed
the exact same
sentiment
when God called him
to lead
the children of Israel
out of Egypt.

Me, Lord?
You want ME
to do WHAT!?

Answering His Call

Both men
felt as though
they were the
wrong guy for the job.

They knew
who they were
and they knew
they fell miserably short
of being what God
needed them to be.

But God,
the one who
created the heavens
and the earth,
had also created them.

He knew them better
than they knew themselves.

Before either of them
had taken
their very first breath,
God had breathed
into them
His plan
for their life.

He knew
the potential
and the possibility
each man possessed.

As I re-read
the passage,
I smiled once again.

This time,
though,
the smile
had my name
written all over it.

Countless times
I, too,
have questioned
the Lord's leading
in my life.

Each time
I am faced
with a new challenge,
or find myself
in uncharted territory,
feeling extremely
out of place
and definitely
out of my comfort zone,
I begin to have
the same conversation
with the Lord.

Are you sure, Lord?
Are you really
calling ME
to do THIS?!

I let the fear
and the uncertainty
and the stress
I am feeling
begin to eat away
at my faith.
Soon,
I find myself
second-guessing

if I am really
where the Lord
has chosen
for me to be.

At times like this,
discerning the Lord's
will for my life
becomes challenging.

God's voice of truth
gets clouded
by my own words of
discouragement,
fear and doubt.

Satan,
always standing by,
waiting for the
itty, bittiest door
of opportunity,
begins to unleash
his arsenal
at me as well.

As the battle rages,
I find myself
looking
for a way out,
a door of escape,
an excuse.

I'm not able Lord!
You've got the wrong girl!

But then..........
then the Lord
draws me to Himself.

In a quiet moment,
as I open His word,
He leads me
to a passage
of indisputable truth,
of divine calling,
of renewed vision.

*"I knew you before
I formed you
in your mother's womb."*
~Jeremiah 1:5, NLT

God knows me better
than I know myself.

Before I, too,
had taken
my very first breath,
He had breathed
into me
His plan for my life.

He knows
the potential
and the possibility
I possess.

In of myself,
I am not able
to do the work
God has created me to do.

Yet,
when I surrender
myself
to the Lord's call
on my life,
I become a vessel

through which others
can see
the work of the Lord.

When I am willing
to be used of God,
through me,
others will see,
God,
I AM,
the Alpha and Omega,
the Beginning and the End!

Each and
every time
this happens,
I smile.

I have a feeling
the Lord smiles, too!

A Sobering Reminder

When was
the last time
you looked
in your rear view mirror
and saw the unwelcome,
flashing red lights
of a police car,
signaling you
to pull over?

You may need
a few minutes
to recall your last encounter;
unfortunately,
mine is still fresh
in my mind.

I was on my way home
a few weeks ago,
when out of nowhere,
a police car
suddenly appeared
in my rear view mirror.

The flashing red lights
not only alerted me
to his presence
but also ushered me
to the side of the road.

A Sobering Reminder

As I stopped the car
and waited
for the policeman
to make his way
to my car,
I replayed
my last few minutes
behind the wheel.

Was I speeding?

No.
I just turned
on to this street.

Did I forget
to use my turn signal
when I made
that last turn?

No.
I remember
hearing the
click, click, click
of the signal
while I sat
at the intersection
waiting for traffic to clear
so I could make my way
to the median.

When I merged
into traffic
did I cut someone off?

No.
I had waited
for all the traffic
to clear

before
I had ventured out
into the street.

I was clueless.

"Good Evening, Ma'am.
Do you know why
I pulled you over?"
he asked matter-of-factly.

"No, Officer," I answered,
"I have no idea."

"Have you had
anything to drink
tonight?"

"No."

"Nothing at all?"

"No."

"I need to see
your driver's license
and your registration."

I reached over,
opened the glove compartment
and quickly located
the requested paper.

"Here is my registration.
My driver's license
is in my purse,
which is in the trunk."

A Sobering Reminder

As he stepped away
from my door,
I exited the car
and made my way
to the trunk of my car,
still wondering
what this was all about.

As I reached
for my purse,
the officer
started to explain
the reason for this stop.

"Ma'am,
you gave me
every reason to believe
you were driving
under the influence.

Unlike most drivers,
you sat at that stop sign
a long time before you
entered the roadway.

Then again,
once in the median,
you waited
before merging
into the westbound lane."

The officer was right.
Well, almost right.
I had taken my time
at that last intersection,
but not because
I had been drinking.

No one was behind me,
so I saw no need
to dart out into
oncoming traffic.

I had opted
to simply
be patient and wait
until all was clear.

"Officer," I answered.
"I can assure you
I haven't been drinking.
I just decided to wait
until all the traffic passed
before I turned onto the road."

"Please have a seat
in your vehicle
and I will be with you
momentarily."

As I waited
for the officer
to return,
I realized
I had caught
this officer's attention
simply because
my behavior
at that intersection
was different
from that
of most other drivers.

Unfortunately,
he thought this difference
was a result
of me tipping the bottle.

A Sobering Reminder

"O.K, Ma'am",
the officer said
as he reappeared
at my window
with my driver's license
and registration in hand,

"You are free to go."

As I pulled away
from the curb,
I thought about this experience

I am a firm believer
that life is full
of teachable moments.

I was pretty sure
God was going
to use this experience
to teach me.

As Christians,
we are called
to live our life
differently
than those
who have not yet
been touched
by the power of Christ.

There should be something
noticeably different about us.

Whether we are
aware of it or not,
people are watching us.

I hadn't seen
the policeman,
but obviously,
he had seen me!

Fortunately,
the officer wasn't able
to arrest me
for drunk driving
because there simply
wasn't any evidence
to substantiate
his concern.
I was sober.

Gently,
I felt the Lord
prompting my heart.

What if this officer
had instead
accused me
of being a Christian?

Would he have found
enough evidence
to arrest me then?

Do my words,
my actions,
the day to day way
I live my life
give testimony
to Christ
alive in me?

What a sobering thought!

A Sobering Reminder

Arriving home,
I pulled into my driveway
and turned off the engine.
Before heading indoors,
I spent a few moments
alone with the Lord,
in the stillness
of the night.

As I opened
my heart
before my Heavenly Father,
He brought the words
of Matthew 5:16
to my mind.

Let your light
shine before others,
so that they may see
your good works,
and give glory to
your Father in heaven.

Yes...
the Lord
had been faithful
to use
a routine traffic stop
to remind me
to live my life
in a way
that is anything
BUT routine.

Where ever I go
and whatever I do,
people are watching.

May the world
see Christ
in me.

A Psalm of My Own

As long as I can remember,
the words to the 23rd Psalms
have been a part of my life.

Having memorized
this passage
as a child,
the words are as
familiar to me
as the Pledge of Allegiance.

Unfortunately,
they were merely that...
words.

Until recently, that is.

After eighteen successful years
in my career of choice,
God began to lead me
in a new direction.

He had a plan.
A Psalms 23 kind of plan.

While circumstances
in my life
seemed out
of my control,

155

I now know
they were never
out of God's control.

He knew
I would never
venture away
from the familiarity
and "safety"
of my job
on my own,
so He allowed
what had always been
a comfortable
and preferred environment,
to become a place
of unrest and misery
for me.

Through each trial
and each unpleasant experience,
God was leading me
away from an old,
familiar place
toward something new.

Thus began
my journey
with the Shepherd.

He led and I followed.

While the way
wasn't always
clear to see,
the love
and faithfulness
of my Heavenly Father
became

A Psalm of My Own

clearer and clearer
with each and every step.

Like David,
I was no longer
simply speaking
the words of his psalm,
but instead
living them.

The Lord is my Shepherd.
I have what I need.

As we walked
together,
God was faithful
to provide
for my every need.

After several years
of searching and seeking,
God led me
to a new place
of employment.

Recently,
a friend asked me
how I liked
my new job.

The words
from my mouth
surprised even me.

"I love my new job.
It is so peaceful
and stress free.
I find myself
laughing again

and thoroughly
enjoying my life.
It's as though
God led me
to a place of rest!"

He lets me
lie down
in green pastures:
he leads me
beside quiet waters.
He renews my life.

From this place
of rest,
I can look back
over my life
and see heartprints
of God's love
every step
of the way.

Through
the ups and down,
the highs and the lows,
He IS there.

Through
the times of plenty and
the times of need,
He IS there.

Through
the times of laughter
and yes,
in the times of sorrow,
He IS there.

A Psalm of My Own

Even when
I go though
the darkest valley,
I fear no danger,
for you are with me;
your rod and your staff -
they comfort me.

You prepare
a table before me
in the presence
of my enemies;
you anoint my head with oil;
my cup overflows.

Truly,
I am blessed.

Daily
my loving Shepherd
has led me
through the valleys,
over the mountain tops,
and beside the still waters.

Through this journey
with Him,
I have never been
out of His care
or without His love.

Like David,
I can rejoice
in my God...
and I can rest
in His guardianship.

The Shepherd knows
the way that is best.

Only goodness
and faithful love
will pursue me
all the days
of my life,
and I will dwell
in the house
of the Lord
as long as I live.
~Psalm 23

Springing Forward

Have you ever wished
you could go back
and completely
redo
a certain episode
or time in your life?

Maybe in anger
you spoke words
that to this day
still separate you
from someone you love.

Maybe you let
a golden opportunity
pass you by
and now
you are haunted
by what might have been.

Maybe you took
a path in life
that has led you
far away
from your
intended destination.

Maybe you simply
let time tick away

without seizing
the moment and
making the most
of each hour
of each day.

Maybe you chose
what didn't matter,
in place of what did.

As much as we
would love a
"do over",
the sad reality
is this:
what is done
is done
and we can't
go back
and undo it.

We can only go forward.

Yet,
how many times
have you and I
gotten
bogged down
in the muddy mess
of regret and guilt
and found our self
idling
instead of
moving on
with our life?

When I opened
my bathroom window
this morning,

Springing Forward

I was surprised
to discover
beautiful blossoms
on our peach tree.

I am always delighted
and amazed in springtime.

Bare trees
become clothed
with beautifully fragrant blossoms.

Birds,
seemingly silent
through the
cold winter months,
now chirp
until their hearts
are content.

And most amazing of all,
the metamorphosis
of the butterfly begins.

All of nature
showcases
the newness
that comes
with the warmth
of the sun
and the birth
of yet another
season of life.

Life goes on.

No matter how
cold the winter,
no matter how

deep the snow;
Spring eventually comes.

The cycle of life
continues
and I am so glad it does.

It is a beautiful reminder
of the new thing
God wants to do
in your life and mine.

Do not remember
the past events;
pay no attention
to the things of old.
Look,
I am about to do
something new;
even now it is coming.
Do you not see it?
Indeed,
I will make a way
in the wilderness,
rivers in the desert.
~Isaiah 43:18-19

Living in the past
only accomplishes
one thing...
keeping us
from living
in the present.

Don't get me wrong.

Wisdom tells us
to learn from the past,
but it in no way

would have us
take up our residence there!

Brothers and sister,
I do not consider myself
to have taken hold of it.
But one thing I do:
Forgetting what is behind,
and reaching forward
to what is ahead,
I pursue as my goal
the prize promised
by God's heavenly call
in Christ Jesus.
~Philippians 3:13,14

Today,
what is
holding you
a prisoner
of the past?

Don't you think
it's time
to let it go?

Can you really afford
to let it keep
stealing your future?

Forget those things
that are behind
and instead
reach for what
is still out
in front of you.

Open your heart
and your life

to receive
the new thing
God is waiting to do...
in and through you!

Our Heavenly Father
has an amazing way
of taking our messes
and turning them
into miracles.

He can take
the ugliness
of our past
and transform it
into something
breathtakingly beautiful.

Just look at what
God can do
in the life
of a caterpillar!

He wants to do that
and so much more
in your life and mine!

We can either
fall back
or we can trust God
and spring forward.

The choice is ours.

Pleasing by Believing

One of my favorite songs
is about
a class of children
with special needs.

While their teacher
taught them their ABC's,
she also shared with them
the love of Jesus.

One day
she told them
of His promise
to come back
and take them
with Him to Heaven.

Well,
from that moment on,
she couldn't keep them
in their seats!

They were always
running to the windows,
pressing their
fingertips and noses
against the windowpane,
looking for Jesus.

HEARTPRINTS OF GOD – The Early Years

If He said
He was coming,
He WAS coming!

Oh,
to have the faith
of these children.

How it must
please our Father's heart
when we take Him
at His word.

If He said it,
He will do it.
No if's, and's or but's
about it.

*Now without faith
it is impossible
to please God,
since the one
who draws near
to him
must believe
that he exists
and that he
rewards those
who seek him.*
~Hebrews 11:6

Without faith
it is impossible
to please God.

We have to
believe that He is
and that He
is a rewarder

of those who
diligently seek Him.

As I look
into my own life,
I have found the moments
that have brought me
the most pleasure
are the ones
where I was
understood
for who I am
and I was taken
at my word.

On the flip side of that,
I can also attest
to the fact
that some
of my most
frustrating and
heartbreaking moments
have been those
when *who I am*
was questioned
or doubted.

We all long
to be someone
others can believe in
and count on.

How much more
God must
desire this
of each
of His children.

Can you imagine
what kind of life
you and I
would be living
at this very moment
if we truly
took the Lord
at His Word?

When I was a child,
I was told
faith
is a lot like
sitting on a chair.

When we sit down,
we do so
in complete confidence
that this
piece of furniture
won't let us down.

We trust
that it will
support us
and hold us up.

Seldom do we
give the chair
a second thought,
much less
a thorough inspection!

Yet,
when it comes
to placing our life
into the hands
of the creator
of the universe,

we hold back,
questioning
and doubting
if He will be there
to hold us up?

I once asked
my class
of first graders
what they were
thankful for.

In the midst
of the usual
flood of responses
such as my bike,
my family, our dog;
one answer
stood high above
the others.

One little boy
simply stated
he was thankful
God was real
and not pretend.

Do you believe
that He is real?

Are you willing
to relinquish the weight
you are carrying
and allow Him
to support you
and hold you up?

Are you ready
to run with me

to the window
of God's heart,
leaving your own
heartprint,
as in eager anticipation,
you look for all
He has promised you?

It is the desire
of my heart
to please my God.

What better way
to do this
than to believe
He is WHO
He says He is
and to know
and trust
He will DO
what He says
He will do.

The Wounds of a Friend

As I gazed
into my mirror,
curling iron in hand,
I was reminded
of a conversation
I had with
a straightforward
second grader
over ten years ago.

I can still hear
his soft spoken voice,
although the words
he spoke
were anything
but soft
to my ears
or my ego.

Each morning,
I would read
a short devotion
to my class.
I was right
in the middle
of the reading
for this particular day,
when out of the
corner of my eye,

I saw a hand
shoot up,
signaling to all
this youngster
had something to say.

And boy, did he!

Not wanting
to deviate
from the spiritual lesson
I was sharing
with these young hearts,
I smiled
at this student,
assuring him
I had seen his hand.

Then,
I did some
hand talking
of my own
as I gave him the
 "hold that thought" sign.

Instead of his
hand going down,
like I had hoped,
his mouth
started
doing the talking
for him.

"Teeeeeeeeeeeeacher,
I have something to tell you!"

"I know, Honey.
Can it please wait
until after we

The Wounds of a Friend

finish our devotion?"

"No, Ma'am.
You are
gonna wanna
hear about this!"

"Ok.
What do you
need to tell me?"

"There is a
gray hair
sticking straight up
on the top
of your head.
I can see it
from way back here!"

He was right
about one thing.

If I did indeed
have a gray hair
standing straight up
on the top
of my head,
I would definitely
want to know
about it.

But me?
A gray hair?
No,
this was where
he had made
his mistake.

"Thank you
for sharing that
with me,
but I think you
might be mistaken.
You see,
I don't have
any gray hair yet, Honey."

"Oh, yes you do!"

The remark came
from a student
sitting
on the opposite side
of the classroom.

 "I see it, too!"

Within seconds,
the room
was flooded
with eyewitness accounts
of a gray hair spotting
in our classroom.

Unfortunately,
all reports
were linking
my head
with this bizarre sighting!

I immediately
headed
for the nearest mirror.

And you know what I saw?

The Wounds of a Friend

Yep!
A gray hair
standing straight up
on the top of my head.

No wonder
this boy
had seen it.

It was proudly
proclaiming
its arrival
in grand fashion.

As it stood tall,
reflecting
every bit of light
in that classroom,
it wasn't any wonder
it had caught
the attention
of every student
in the room.

After all,
who could miss
THAT?!

Uhhhhhh,
obviously me.
That's who.

Until this
honest,
straightforward
little boy
had so bluntly
pointed it out to me,
I had been

totally oblivious to it.

But don't just
listen
to God's word.
You must do
what it says.
Otherwise,
you are only
fooling yourselves.
For if you
listen to the word
and don't obey,
it is like
glancing
at your face
in a mirror.
You see yourself,
walk away,
and forget
what you look like.
~James 1:22-24, NLT

I had looked
in my mirror
that very morning
and had failed
to see
what others
could see
so plainly.

I wonder
how many times
I have looked
at my reflection
through the pages
of God's Word,
only to be

The Wounds of a Friend

blinded
to my own sins.

How often
has my pride
kept me
completely
in the dark
about my
true spiritual condition,
while those around me
can spot my need
for repentance
a mile away?

The truth hurts
and is never
easy on
our ears,
our ego
or our heart,
and yet
how we should
covet
the honest words
of a faithful friend.

The words of truth
that bring confession,
dropping us
to our knees
and into the hands
of our forgiving God.

Nathan
was that
kind of friend
to David.

Thinking his
sin of adultery
with Bathsheba
and the consequential
prearranged murder
of her husband
on the battle field
were well hidden
and out of sight,
Nathan
confronted him
with words that cut
to the very heart
of David.

"You are that man!"

David confessed.
God forgave.
Then David
continued his journey,
pursuing
the heart of God.

The truth hurts.
There is no
getting around that.
But,
truth also
sets us free.

The pain
has a
distinct purpose;
to open our eyes
to the real us,
and our need
for a real God.

Iron sharpens iron,
and one person
sharpens another.
  ~Proverbs 27:17

When truth
is given to us,
we have a choice
to make.

We can
resist it
and in anger
turn away from it.

Or,
like David,
we can run to it,
embrace it,
be broken by it,
and be all
the closer to God
for it.

Faithful are
the wounds
of a friend;
but the kisses
of an enemy
are deceitful.
~Proverbs 27:6, NKJV

An Answer to Prayer

Just the other day,
God used me
to answer a prayer.

Me!

Imagine that.

Now,
I know God
uses each of us,
in many ways,
on any given day,
to be an
answer to prayer,
but on this day,
it was the last thing
I would have
ever expected
God to do.

You see,
on this particular day,
my thoughts and actions
had been anything
but pleasing
to God.

An Answer to Prayer

From the moment
my alarm had
jolted
me awake,
my grumbling
and complaining
had started.

Before my feet
even had a chance
to hit the floor,
my mouth
had started
groaning to God
about this,
and whining to God
about that.

By the time
I made it
to the shower,
my pity party
was in full swing.

I wish I could say
a nice hot shower
did the trick,
and before long
I was rejoicing
in this new day
that the Lord had made,
but unfortunately,
that wasn't the case.

It seemed the
more I moaned,
the more I found
to moan about.

By the time
I left for work,
I was
singing the blues
better than B.B. King!

And it didn't stop there.

The events
of the day
kept giving me more
to complain about.

I couldn't believe
what a
horrible,
rotten,
no good day
I was having.

Then,
to top it all off,
I found myself
sitting in traffic
at a railroad crossing.

With nothing
to do
but wait,
I began to watch
the activity
in a store parking lot
to my left.

That's when it happened.

I spotted my then
eighty-four year old
father-in-law

184

An Answer to Prayer

attempting
to change a flat tire
on his truck.

When the way
was clear,
I maneuvered
my way over
to where he was parked.

As soon as he
saw me pull up,
a look of relief
flooded his face.

"Oh, Stacy!
I can't believe it's you.
I just prayed God
would send
someone to help me
and here you are.
You are the answer
to my prayer!"

God, how could you?

How could you
possibly
have chosen ME
to be the one
to bless
this dear man today?

How could I be
the answer
to a prayer
spoken in desperation,
when my own lips
were so desperately

far from you
today?

How could you
even think
to use me
when I have
been acting
in a way
so undeserving
of this honor?

In spite of
my thoughts,
my actions
and my lousy,
no good for nothing attitude,
God used me.

In spite of
what I had done and
what I had said,
God used me.

In spite of who I am,
God used me.

But why?
Why would He
choose
to do that?

Because,
it's not about me....
it's about Him.

Now we have
this treasure
in clay jars,

186

An Answer to Prayer

so that this
extraordinary power
may be from God
and not from us.
~2 Corinthians 4:7

The sad truth is,
even on a "good day",
when my words
and my thoughts
bring a smile
to my Father's face,
the only good
in me,
is still Him.

Who I am
is simply
a vessel that,
amazingly,
God chooses
to work through
to touch others
with His love,
and in this case,
His provision.

I phoned my husband,
and soon,
my father-in-law and I
were each back
on the road again
and headed back into
the rest of our day.

As I drove,
I bowed my heart
before the
Lover of my soul.

Through words
of confession
and repentance,
mingled with tears
of shame and regret,
I felt God's
unconditional love
flood my heart.

I was chosen
to be someone's
answer to prayer,
and yet I
couldn't help believing
God has used
this encounter
to answer a prayer
of my own.

Just like my father-in-law,
I needed my God
to rescue me.

Depression was
sucking the life
out of my day
and out of my heart,
yet before I had even
sought the Lord
for a way of escape
from this cruel prison,
He had answered.

God, how could you?
How could you
be so beautiful to me?

As I continued my day,
I found myself

humming
a brand new tune.

A melody of
grace,
forgiveness
and joy!

Why,
I could hardly believe
the beautiful day
I was having!

Advice for a Hurting Heart

As I sit here
writing this,
I am sipping
on a Dr. Pepper float.

Yet as yummy
and delicious
as this creamy,
refreshing drink is,
I am still
finding it hard
to swallow the hurt
I experienced earlier
this morning.

Hence,
the reason
for this mid-afternoon splurge.

Silly as it sounds,
I actually hoped
this ice cream treat
would sweeten
the sour feeling
I have been
carrying around
in my heart all day.

WRONG!

Advice for a Hurting Heart

Why is it
when the world
hits us and kicks us
and bruises our very soul,
we head straight back
into the world
in search of the healing
we are so desperately
in need of?

It makes no sense
to me and yet,
here I sit
with a straw
in my mouth,
sucking away
at this frozen concoction
as though
my very heart
depended on it.

No wonder I feel deflated.
And taken advantage of.

After slurping
my way
to the bottom
of my treat,
I am still left
with a hurting heart
and a loaded question
for God.

God,
how can I
pour out myself
so as to be
used by YOU
without being used

by the very one
I am pouring
myself out to?

I told you
it was
a loaded question.

I wish I could say
this is the first time
I have sought God
for an answer
to this life-long dilemma,
but it isn't.

For most of my life,
I have bent over
backward
to be God's
hands and feet
to a hurting world,
often at my own expense.

At times,
the outpouring
of my heart
has been
gently received
and upheld
with sincerest appreciation.

Other times,
however,
my giving heart
has been trampled on,
greedily taken from,
and squandered,
with no regret
and no shame.

Advice for a Hurting Heart

Such was the case today.

And it hurts.

How can I be
used by God
without being used?

As a Christian,
I suppose
we could simply
chalk up
"being taken
advantage of"
as an
"occupational hazard".

It just comes
with the title
of Christian.

After all,
we are called
to be partakers
of Christ's suffering.

No one was more
used and abused
than our precious Lord.

And yet,
does God really
want or expect us
to allow others
to use our heart
for their own selfish gain?

As odd as it may seem,
I think God gave me

a glimpse into His answer
as my husband and I
were finishing our lunch today.

It was one of
those rare days
when our schedules
coincided
and we were able
to meet together
for a moment
and a meal.

As my husband
reached for the check,
he handed me
a fortune cookie.

While I don't believe
in fortune cookies,
I do believe,
if we have
ears to hear and
eyes to see,
our God
can and will
speak to us
through the events
of our day.

As I read
the words written
on the tiny slip of paper
hiding in this simple dessert,
I tenderly heard
the wisdom
of my loving Heavenly Father.

Advice for a Hurting Heart

It is a silly fish
that is caught twice
with the same bait.

God has
called us to give...
to give
with our whole heart.

However,
if after we give,
our eyes and our heart
are opened to see
the true intent
of the recipient
of our heart,
and it is evil in nature,
then God would have us
learn from this
and head
in a new direction,
away from this abuse.

We don't need
to fight back.

We don't need
to retaliate.

Most of all,
we don't need
to go back for more.

We simply need
to learn
from this experience
and then,
move on.

"Look,
I'm sending you out
like sheep among wolves.
Therefore be as
shrewd as serpents and
as innocent as doves."
~Matthew 10:16

As I toss my
empty cup and straw
into the trash,
I delicately place
my hurting heart
into the nail scarred hands
of Jesus.

He knows how I feel.
He has been there, too.

As I release
this hurt
through the gift
of forgiveness,
He will bring
the healing I need.

Tomorrow is a new day.
A brand new day
to go out
and touch the world
with the love
of my Heavenly Father.

May I never stop being
His hands and His feet.

May I never let my heart
become so calloused
it refuses to give.

196

Advice for a Hurting Heart

May I always
run to my Father
when I am hurting.

May my heart
always rejoice
in service to my God.

Tears of Joy

As I child,
I never really
liked
playing Hide-n-Seek.

Well,
that's not
entirely true.

I thoroughly
enjoyed hiding,
but when it came
my time
to do the seeking,
I would always suggest
a game of Hopscotch.

Don't get me wrong.
I'm more than willing
to hold up my end
of a game.
If I hide,
I need to take
my turn seeking.
I get that.

But for some
odd reason,
not knowing

where to look,
made me feel
anxious and uneasy.

Sherlock Holmes,
I am not,
and I don't get
the tiniest bit
of pleasure
out of a "good" mystery.

If I am looking for something,
or in this case,
someone,
I want to know
exactly where to look.

I want a map
with a big,
bright red "X"
marking the spot.

But,
hide-n-seek
doesn't work that way.
It's all about the hunt;
followed by
the excitement you feel
when you discover
your friend hiding
in the last place
you would ever
have thought to look.

Once I gave
my heart to Christ
and His precious
Holy Spirit
came to live inside me,

I began to discover
the fruit of the Spirit
in my life.

As I allowed
the Spirit
to take control,
love,
peace,
patience,
kindness,
goodness,
faithfulness,
gentleness
and self-control
became evident
at different times
and places
in my Christian walk.

Joy,
however,
seemed to be
hiding from me.

But how could this be?

Wasn't
it
supposed to be
in my life, too?

Although separate
and unique,
these characteristics
of Christ
are one.
After all,
they are known

as the fruit of the Spirit,
not the fruits of the spirit.

So...where was my joy?

Believe it or not,
when I finally found it,
it was in the
last place
I would ever
have thought to look.

Following Christ,
I soon discovered,
is not an easy thing to do.

This spiritual journey
requires much
from those
who would choose
to walk the walk,
and not simply
talk the talk.

To be true
followers of Christ,
we must be willing
to give Christ
our all -
and this
requires sacrifice,
and death.

Yes, even death.

Then he said to them all,
"If anyone wants
to follow after me,
let him deny himself,

take up his cross daily,
and follow me. "
Luke 9:23

In order for Christ
to live fully
in and through me,
I must die.
You must die, too.

As children of the
Most High God,
we are called upon
to take up
our cross daily,
denying self
and surrendering all
to God.

This process of becoming
a new creature in Christ
is excruciatingly painful.

Death never comes
without tears of sorrow.

Those who
sow in tears
will reap
with shouts of joy.
~ Psalm 126:5

Tears.

What an
unlikely place
to discover my joy,
and yet,
that is exactly where

I keep finding it.

As I surrender
my will
to the will
of my Father,
I pass through
a valley of tears.

Yet,
on the other side
of this dark place,
I discover true joy.

*You rejoice in this,
even though now
for a short time,
if necessary,
you suffer grief
in various trials
so that the
proven character
of your faith -
more valuable
than gold which,
though perishable,
is refined by fire -
may result in praise,
glory, and honor
at the revelation
of Jesus Christ.*

*Though you
have not seen him,
you love him;
though not seeing him now,
you believe in him,
and you rejoice
with inexpressible*

and glorious joy.
~1 Peter 1:6-8

Unlike the game
of Hide-n-Seek,
God has been
faithful
to map out
the way for us.

The blood stained
cross of Calvary
clearly
marks the spot
where our joy
is found.

Looking unto Jesus,
the author and
finisher of our faith,
who for the joy
that was set before Him
endured the cross,
despising the shame,
and has sat down
at the right hand
of the throne of God.
~Hebrews 12:2 NKJV

Imagine the thrill
of my discovery
when I finally found
God's precious
gift of joy
in my tears
of surrender.

Kneeling
at the foot

of the cross,
I exchange
my tears of sorrow
for tears of joy.

It is here,
I find joy
unspeakable.

Stand

I have a question for you.

What do you do
when life
doesn't make sense?

When a loved one
is tragically killed
in a car accident?

When your doctor says,
"It's cancer".

When you are
suddenly
laid off from work?

When your dream dies?

When you are left
with a million questions
and not one single answer?

What do you do?

You stand.

That's what you do.

It's as simple
and as critical
as that.

For some reason,
when we find our self
experiencing
a trial or hardship,
our humanness demands
to know why.

At first,
our questions
are almost always
me-centered.

Why me?

Why did
this
have to happen
to me?

What did
I do
to deserve this?

Then,
God
gets thrown
in to the questioning.

Why would
God
allow this
to happen?

Why would
a God of love

let me suffer
like this?

Why didn't
God
step in
and do something
to stop this?

More times than not,
our questioning
only leads us
to feelings of
confusion,
anger,
or despondency,
not the answer
we are so
desperately seeking.

In our need
to find answers,
we often
find our self
overlooking
or forgetting
what we do know,
in search of
that which we
may never know,
at least not
on this side of Heaven.

In times like these,
we need
to stop trying
to understand
and to simply
stand.

Stand

At a very
low point
in my life,
I found myself
playing the
"why" game
with God.

Day in
and day out
I kept pleading
with Him
for an answer.

I believed
if I could just
understand
the "why"
behind
what was happening,
I would be able
to deal with it,
accept it
and move on.

God remained silent.

For months,
I wrestled
with my emotions
and my God.

Finally,
one day
God did speak.

*"Stacy,
if you keep
trying*

*to figure out
the why,
if you keep
demanding
to understand this,
you are going
to remain
frustrated and distant
from Me.*

*Your need
to understand
is going to
take you under!*

*Simply stand
on what you
do know.*

*You know
I am
all love,
all the time
and you can trust Me
with your very life.*

*You know
I want
only the best for you
and I am always
working everything
out for your good
and My glory.*

*Quit trying to
understand this.
Instead,
stand on
who I am*

and the promises
I have made to you."

While this
word from God
wasn't the answer
to my question,
and certainly
not the answer
I was looking for,
I found it to be
the answer to my peace.

Today
is the need
to know why
tormenting your mind
and stealing your peace?

Do you feel
as though
you are drowning
in a sea of questions?

Are you tired
of the struggle
to keep your faith
above water
and your eyes
on God,
only to get
pulled under
by the current of
confusion,
doubt
and anger
time and time again?

Why not
choose instead
to stand
on the foundation
of God's
unfailing love
for you?

You may
have to
surrender
your need
to know why,
but the peace
you will discover
in its place
will be more
than worth it.

More importantly,
your continued
trust and faith
in God
depends on it.

Today,
right now,
stand on
what you do know.

God loves me.

God is working
all things
for my good
and for His glory.

God will
never leave me

nor forsake me.

God is
all love,
all the time.

God can
be trusted
with my very life.

If you allow
these truths
to be the
foundation
on which you
place your faith,
the questions of life
will never be able
to pull you under.

Take your stand,
and do it today!

Pitfalls, Potholes, and a Heavenly Perspective

It had been
one of those days!
Actually,
if I'm truthful,
I would have to admit
It had been one those weeks!

You know the kind
I'm talking about.

The kind
that leaves you
exhausted,
frustrated
and ready to give up.

Thankfully,
nothing major
had happened to me.

Surprisingly enough,
it had been
the little,
dare I say,
ordinary things of life
that somehow
banded together

Pitfalls, Potholes, and a Heavenly Perspective

to wreak havoc
on my week
and my emotions.

Isn't it amazing
how simple
every day things
like finding your car keys
or balancing your checkbook
can turn your whole day
upside down
and send you into a tail spin?

And yes,
I realize
it's not what's
happening
that's the problem.

It's my reaction to it.

The simple fact
that I allow these
seemingly small,
insignificant things
in my life
to become
bigger than life
frustrates me
beyond words.

Before I know it,
I am taking
a detour
paved with
anger,
anxiety
and frustration.

HEARTPRINTS OF GOD – The Early Years

How I wish
I could bypass
this emotional trip
altogether
and simply
deal with it
and move on.

Which brings me
to Driver's Ed. 101.

When I was first
learning to drive,
I got some
excellent advice
from my father.

One day,
as we were
cruising down
a dirt road
out in the country,
I found myself
struggling
to keep the car
moving in a straight,
forward direction.

I would wander
to the left,
then meander
off to the right,
only to drift left again.

Driving straight
turned out to be
a lot harder
than I thought.

Pitfalls, Potholes, and a Heavenly Perspective

After several miles
of crisscrossing
back and forth
across this road,
my father gently spoke
words of wisdom.

"Quit staring
at the hood
of the car
and focusing
all your attention
on what's directly
in front of you.
Instead,
look past it
and concentrate
on where you are going."

I told you
my Daddy was wise.

I took his advice
(I am my
father's daughter,
after all)
and soon,
I was driving
like a pro!

No more
careening
back and forth
across the road
for this girl.

Now I was wheeling
and dealing
and finally getting

somewhere!

Which brings me
back to today
and this week.

Once again,
I found myself
veering of course.

Instead of looking
at the big picture,
I allowed these
minor inconveniences
to become
my focal point.

Where are those keys hiding?
Why aren't these numbers adding up?
Why is life so tough?

With each question,
I found myself
heading toward
Misery Lane,
and straight for
Pity Party Parkway.

Aaaay yi yi!

How quickly
I forget
the words
of my father...
and the words of Paul.

For our present
troubles are small
and won't last very long.

218

Pitfalls, Potholes, and a Heavenly Perspective

Yet they produce
for us a glory
that vastly outweighs them
and will last forever!

So we don't look
at the troubles
we can see now;
rather,
we fix our gaze
on things that
cannot be seen.

For the things
we see now
will soon be gone,
but the things
we cannot see
will last forever.
~ 2 Corinthians 4:17-18, NLT

Let's face it.

As we journey
through life,
there are sure to be
some potholes
waiting around the bend.

It's how we
purposely choose
to react
to these potholes
that makes
all the difference.

The choice is up to us.

After all,
we are the ones
in the driver's seat,
right?!

We can allow
these "light afflictions"
to throw us
off course,
or worse yet,
stop us in our tracks
or we can simply
cruise right on
around them
and keep
on keeping on.

Lord, What Would You Have Me to Do?

The words she spoke
still ring in my ears;
the pleas she made
still echo in my heart.

As I sat listening
to this missionary
tell of the places
God had taken her
and the experiences
she had witnessed,
her words
opened my heart
to a world in need.

They awakened
a yearning
in my soul
that has left me asking,
*"Lord,
what would You
have ME to do?"*

As this women of faith
spoke of God's call
on her life,
she smiled.

She was,
after all,
an ambassador*
for Christ
(* 2 Corinthians 5:20),
a title she wore
with both pride
and utmost humility.

Her call
had taken her
far from the
comforts of her
quaint little home
and far beyond
the borders
of her homeland.

It was not
the plan
she would have
chosen for her life,
and yet
it was exactly
the life
she was meant
to live.

She had been
obedient to follow
God's leading
and He had been
faithful to accompany her
every step of the way.

She told of
numerous trips
to various countries.

Lord, What Would You Have Me to Do?

She shared
story after story
of God's provision
and His constant protection.

She also shared
testimony after testimony
of souls being won
for the Kingdom.

It was exhilarating
to listen to these
firsthand accounts
of God's power
and His presence.

Toward the end
of her talk,
she told
of her travels
to a country
I cannot pronounce,
much less spell.

The conditions
were primitive.
The villages,
small and scattered.
The people,
in great need.

One day,
as they traveled
the hot, dusty road
from one village
to the next,
they stopped
at a small, roadside stand.

Here,
they hoped to find
some fresh water,
along with fresh produce
and some much needed refreshment.

To their surprise,
not only did
this poor vendor
have water
and fresh produce,
he also had cans
of Coca Cola...
COCA COLA!

As the
ambassador of Christ
relived this experience,
her smile faded
and tears
filled her eyes.

As she had
traveled this country,
she had not seen
one church
or one Bible.

There was no
visible evidence
to indicate anyone
had gone before her
in this pursuit
to share the
good news of Christ.

Obviously,
the Coca Cola Corporation
had made the effort

Lord, What Would You Have Me to Do?

to go to this country
and introduce these people
to their product,
a beverage
they have touted
to the world
as the "real thing".

Christians,
however,
had yet to lead
these precious people
to the living water,
and the one real God!

They had Coca Cola,
but they didn't have Jesus.

Her tears
soon became mine.

If a corporation
is willing to venture
to faraway places
in hopes
of increasing
the value of their company,
shouldn't we,
as ambassadors of Christ,
be willing to do
whatever it takes
to bring the people
of the world
the living hope?

Shouldn't we
be willing
to share with them
that which

is of eternal value?

They don't need coke.
They need Christ.

But how will they know
unless someone
is willing to tell them?

For everyone who calls
on the name of the Lord
will be saved.
But how can they
call on him
to save them
unless they
believe in him?

And how can they
believe in him
if they have never
heard about him?

And how can they
hear about him
unless someone tells them?
And how will anyone
go and tell them
without being sent?

That is why
the Scriptures say,
"How beautiful are
the feet of messengers
who bring good news!"
~Romans 10:13-15, NLT

The words she spoke
still ring in my ears;

Lord, What Would You Have Me to Do?

the pleas she made
still echo in my heart.

As I sit writing
about this missionary
and the places God
has taken her
and the experiences
she has witnessed,
I pray her words
open your heart
to a world in need.

I pray they awaken
a yearning
in your soul
that leaves you asking,
"Lord,
what would You
have ME to do? "

My Misplaced "I"

The other day
I was busily
typing away;
my fingers
flying across
my keyboard
in a meager attempt
to keep up
with my runaway thoughts.

As new words
and sentences
appeared
on my screen,
I suddenly realized
I had made
a typo.

A HUGE TYPO!

A typo that
would have gone
unnoticed
by spellcheck,
but not by
anyone reading
the finished product!

This typo changed everything!

My Misplaced "I"

Isn't it amazing
how one
simple letter,
when placed
in the wrong position,
can change
the entire meaning
of a word?

As I sat there
looking at this
new word
I had typed
by mistake,
God began
to speak
to my heart.

I soon
discovered
myself
shaking my head
and smiling.

God is so amazing.
I never cease
to be amazed
at the way
He goes
to any length
to mold me
and shape me
and make me
more like Him.

I have a feeling
He was smiling
right along with me.

Untied.

This is the word
I found myself
looking at.

Untied
- a word that means
to loose or unfasten.

I certainly
had not intended
to type this word
and to convey
this meaning.

Quite the opposite,
in fact.

United.

This is the word
I had meant to type.

United
- a word that means
to become joined together
or combined form a single whole

When I
looked closely,
I realized
the meanings
of these two words
change dramatically
depending on
where
one letter
is positioned

in the word.

Upon further
examination,
I discovered
the letter
capable
of loosening something
that had previously
been joined together
was none other
than the letter "i".

Isn't that
the way
it always is?

*Because of the
privilege and authority
God has given me,
I give each of you
this warning:
Don't think
you are better
than you really are.*

*Be honest
in your evaluation
of yourselves,
measuring yourselves
by the faith
God has given us.*
~Romans 12:3, NLT

If I want my life
to be united
with Christ,
I have to allow
the Holy Spirit

231

to keep me
in my proper place,
under God's Kingship
and surrendered
to His authority
in my life.

Like John
in John 3:30,
He must increase,
but I must decrease.

Otherwise,
everything
is going to come
unraveled and untied.

When Christ
is not at the
center of my life,
everything else
is off balance
and becomes
topsy turvy.

Are you looking
for stability
in your life?

Are you wondering
why life
just seems
to keep
coming undone
even though
you are doing
your best
to keep it all together?

My Misplaced "I"

Look closely.

Maybe like me,
you have
your "I"
in the wrong place.

Sculpted by a Child

Today,
I had the
privilege
of attending
an end-of-the-year
awards ceremony
at a local elementary school.

As I saw the children
go forward
to receive their awards
and the proud look
on the faces
of the parents
standing high
above the crowd,
camera in hand,
it reminded me
of another ceremony
I attended a year ago last May.

This celebration
was a preschool graduation;
a momentous occasion
to be sure!

Every one
was dressed
in their finest attire

and spirits were high.

Each class
had a special part
in the program,
from the very young
two year olds
to the growing-up-quick
five year olds
who made up
the graduating class.

As I watched
from my seat,
parents watched through
their camcorders,
trying to capture
this never-to come-again
moment in time.

The program was entitled,
"Our God is SO Big!"

What a delight
to celebrate
this truth
with ones
who were still
so little.

The children
sang and danced.

When they finished,
there was no denying
we serve a HUGE God.

There was also
undeniable evidence
that we can learn
some valuable,
life changing lessons
from children.

Lesson # 1:
Bring Special Attention to the Important People
in Your Life by Sharing the Spotlight

Inevitably,
once a child
arrived up
on the big stage,
he or she
would begin
searching the sea
of faces
in the audience.

When at last
the prized person
was spotted,
be it their
Mom, Dad,
brother, sister,
grandmother, grandfather,
aunt, uncle,
a friend next door,
or even the mailman,
the proud child
would wave exuberantly
and in a voice
loud enough
for even the people
on the back row
to hear,
say "HI!"

Sometimes,
the proud performer
would even
call out
the person's name
or declare
with uninhibited enthusiasm,
"LOOK!
That's my Mommy!
That's my Daddy!
That's my Nana!
That's my Papa!"

As the audience
turned their heads
in the direction
of the child's gaze,
these two people,
for one brief moment,
shared the spotlight together.

A room apart,
but heart to heart.

Lesson # 2:
Be Proud of Who God Made You to Be!

As the three year olds
took the stage,
one girl in particular,
took the cake!

She had on a
beautiful, pink,
polka dot dress.

As she was
swinging
to the beat

of the song
they were singing,
she discovered
a wonderful secret
about her dress.

If she swung
to the left
and then back again
to the right
with enough pizazz,
the ends
would flare out.

It wasn't long
before she had
mastered
this movement
and went
for the grand finale -
a full circle!

It was obvious
she was thrilled
with this new
found skill
and before long,
she was spinning
all across the stage.

Bursting with
pride and joy,
she yelled out...
"Look at me!
Look at me!
I'm boootiful!"

And she was,
but her dress

had nothing
to do with it.

It was
the freedom
she felt,
the freedom
to be her
and to enjoy
being her
that was beautiful.

As I sat there
that evening,
trying to
take it all in,
I found myself
wanting to be
just like these
precious little ones.

*Oh to be so in love
and so proud
of the people
in my life that,
when the spotlight
is on me,
I direct
the attention
of others
to them instead.*

*Lord,
help me to be
ever mindful
of the people
You have placed
in my life.*

*Let me
never forget
that they are
a huge reason
behind
why I am
where I am today.*

*Let me always
give credit
where credit is due
and may I never be
too proud,
too embarrassed or
too self-absorbed
to share
the moments of my life
with the people I love.*

*In humility
and with
uninhibited enthusiasm,
may my life
always exclaim
"LOOK! That's my God!"*

*Oh to be
so in love
with who
you made me
to be
that I showcase
the beauty
of your workmanship
with sheer delight
and reckless abandon.*

*Your word declares
I am fearfully*

Sculpted by a Child

and wonderfully made.
As I swing
to the beat
of my life,
may I daily
discover
the beauty
You have
placed in me.

May I always
dance and revel
in your creative touch,
daily embracing
the uniqueness of me.

As I live my life
with pizazz,
boldly pronouncing,
"I'm beautiful!",
may the beauty
others see,
be the freedom
I have found in you.

Sometimes –
sometimes if
you are lucky -
your heart
is sculpted
by the heart
of a child.

The Faith of a Child

My very first
year of teaching
found me
at a Christian school
in Wisconsin.

(Did I happen
to mention
it was a
one-room
Christian school?!)

My assignment -
teach eighteen students,
from first grade
up to the eighth grade.

It was an amazing year.
I know I owe
the success
of my career
to these vivacious,
talented,
awesome children -
all adults now!

These students
taught me well.

The Faith of a Child

One lesson
in particular
came from a little
second grade girl
named Crystal.

Crystal had
mixed feelings
about school.
She was thrilled
to be part
of our class,
just not excited
to be part
of the second grade.

You see,
she WAS
the second grade.

All the other grades
I taught had
at least two children,
but not second grade.
Crystal was the
only one
in this grade level.

Several weeks
into the school year,
Crystal came walking
up to my desk
with a smile
as bright as she was.
She had an idea
and couldn't wait
to share it with me.

HEARTPRINTS OF GOD – The Early Years

Her idea -
pray God would
bring another family
to our school -
a family who had
a second grader.

From that moment on,
each time we prayed,
Crystal asked God
for another second grader.

It was obvious
she wasn't concerned
about if...
only when and who.

The more we prayed,
the more excited she got.
The more excited she got,
the more anxious
I started to feel.

I knew God
was able
to answer
the prayer
of this sweet,
little heart,
but would He?

What if He choice not to?

What would I tell Crystal?

The months passed quickly
and soon we dismissed
for Christmas vacation.

The Faith of a Child

When school
resumed
in January,
we welcomed
a new family
to our class.
This family had
four children
and it just so
happened
one of them
was a second grader
named Jamie.

Did I mention
Crystal's request
was not only
for a second grader,
but for a second grader
who was also a girl?!

Jamie fit
Crystal's prayer
to a tee!

I was so excited!

God had heard
and answered
the prayer
of this little girl!

Crystal,
on the other hand,
showed no emotion.

She knew
all along
God was going

to send someone
and her
simple response was,
"Hi! My name is Crystal.
I knew you were coming
and I am glad
you are finally here."

The Problem With No

As I phoned
my husband
on my way home
from work,
it was obvious
to his listening heart
that something
was bothering me.

"What's wrong?"
he asked.

"Oh, nothing,"
I replied.

"Are you sure?"
he inquired further.

"I guess I'm just
upset at myself,"
I finally admitted.

"Why?
What did you do?"

"I agreed
to help out
with an event
in the park

this weekend."

"And you
don't really want
to do it, do you?"

"NO!" I answered.

"You are just going
to have to learn
to say no, Beautiful."

"Oh, I can say no."
I shot back.
"But for some
odd reason,
when I say it,
it is always followed
by the word problem.
You know, as in,
'Oh sure, no problem'."

"Well, see,"
he said triumphantly.
"That's your problem.
You need to
just leave it
at no."

We ended
our conversation
and I continued
my drive home.

Oh,
if only
it were
that easy.

The Problem With No

If only
I could
say no.

Why is it
when someone
asks me to do something,
I always feel
compelled
to say yes?

The light
at the upcoming
intersection
turned yellow
and the traffic
slowed to a stop.

It's the guilt.
That's what it is.
If I say no,
I feel so guilty,
not to mention
selfish.
I always
end up feeling
like I'm a
horrible person.

The light now green,
I shifted into gear
and continued
my commute.

Lord,
You have
called us
to be servants.

HEARTPRINTS OF GOD – The Early Years

You want us
to be Your hands
and Your feet
to a world in need.
You want us
to say yes,
don't you?

Once again,
the traffic slowed.
Orange construction barrels
now herded us
into a single lane.
Slowly the
parade of cars
crept through
the work zone.

Lord,
I'm so torn inside.
I want to help people.
I really do.
Yet,
at the same time,
I honestly don't.

Sometimes,
I just want to do
something for me.

How selfish is that!

I feel guilty if I say no,
but then when I say yes,
I feel resentful.

No matter what I do,
I never seem to win.

The Problem With No

Please Lord.
I need Your help.
Show me the right way...
Your way.

Having no other option,
I continued to follow
the car ahead of me
as we slowly meandered
our way through
this work in progress.

What's that, Lord?
What did you say?

Yes, I remember.
You told us
to love our neighbor
as we love our self.

I'm trying to love
my neighbor, Lord.
That's why
I always say yes.

What, Lord?

Myself?

Do I love myself
like I love
my neighbor?

The lane
I was driving on
now became uneven,
causing my car
to tilt to the right.

HEARTPRINTS OF GOD – The Early Years

Driving at this
new angle
felt awkward
and made me
feel strangely
uncomfortable.

What's that, Lord?

Hum...yes,
I hate to admit it,
but You're right.

When I say yes,
I'm only giving
lip service,
and not truly
loving from my heart.

My mouth says
"no problem",
but my heart
doesn't agree.

But wait, Lord.
What does this
have to do
with me
loving myself?

Soon,
the all too familiar
pavement ended
and we ventured
forward
over rough, dusty terrain.

The previous
pavement

had been
completely removed,
allowing the workers
to prepare this area
for new improved lanes
that would be wider
and free of potholes.

Oh, I see Lord.
It's about finding
a balance,
isn't it?

You have
commanded me
to love my neighbor,
but at the same time,
you have also
commanded me
to love myself.

You want my love
to be true...
both to others
and myself.

Finally,
we reached the end
of the work zone.

Once again,
I found myself
on smooth,
even pavement
and driving at ease.

As I continued
my commute,
I realized the Lord

had been lovingly
guiding me through
the confusion
in my heart.

As I arrived home,
my husband
came out
to greet me.

"Wow!"
he exclaimed.
"Why the
big smile
on your face?
Last time
I talked to you,
you were anything
but happy."

"Let's just say
I had a great
commute home,"
I answered.

"Didn't you have
to drive through
that new construction zone?
That section
of the road
is a mess!"

"Yep,
but you
know what?
Surprisingly,
it turned out to be
"no problem",
after all."

The Testing Times of Life

*"Yet he knows
the way I have taken;
when he has tested me,
I will emerge as pure gold."*
~ Job 23:10

"All right, class.
I need everyone
to clear the top
of his or her desk.
Today,
we are having
a pop quiz."

Aah....a pop quiz.
Unlike other tests,
this is a test
that just "pops up",
totally unexpected
and totally unplanned for.

As a student,
whenever I heard
these instructions
from my teacher,
I always started
to feel anxious
and in some ways,

255

tricked.

I hadn't been
warned
of this test
ahead of time
and as a result,
I hadn't
taken the time
to prepare.
I hadn't studied.
I simply wasn't ready.

But... ready or not,
the test landed
on my desk.

Yesterday,
I was surprised
with a pop quiz.
It didn't come
in the usual way -
as a paper
placed on my desk.

No,
this test
popped into
my life
when I found myself
confronted
by an angry person.

Just yesterday,
I started my day
by meditating
on countless scriptures
in God's Word
that pertain to peace.

The Testing Times of Life

When I walked
out my door
yesterday morning,
I was walking in peace.

Then......
all that changed.
As this woman
attacked me
with bitter words,
I felt anything
but peaceful.

Oh,
you'll be happy
to know
on the outside,
I remained
calm, cool
and collected.
I responded in love
and tried to
defuse her anger
in a gentle way.

But.....
on the inside......
I was a mess!

Anger,
hurt,
resentment,
frustration.

All of these
emotions
and about
a zillion more
were having

their own
"private" war.

When this "battle"
was over,
my peace was gone.

For the next
couple of hours,
I kept replaying
the scene in my mind.

What just happened there?

How could that have just happened?

Today,
of all days,
I was going
to walk in peace.

I was all
"peaced up"
when I had left my home.

But,
where was
my peace now?

How come
my peace
hadn't survived
this altercation?

Wasn't that the
whole purpose
of peace
in the first place?

Then,
it hit me.

POP QUIZ!

Only this
is one test
I should
have passed
with flying colors.

I knew
all the verses
about peace.
I was prepared.
I had studied
for this one.

Yet,
when the
test came,
I failed.

Why?

It is one thing
to know something.
It is something
entirely different
to apply
this knowledge
and make it
who you are.

Teachers often
use testing
as a means
to determine
whether or not

a child
has mastered
a skill or discipline.

A wise teacher
will use not one,
but multiple tests,
to gauge the level
of understanding
in the student.

It is not enough
to simply
memorize facts,
repeat rules,
or circle A, B, C, or D.

A student must
apply the knowledge
in order to
gain the wisdom.
The child must
take the information
and then
use it,
apply it,
make it work.

I had the information,
but now
I was being
called upon
to use this information,
to apply it,
to make it work.

Peace isn't simply
something we can
merely talk about.

The Testing Times of Life

It is something
we need to
put into practice
in our daily lives.

If we don't,
what's the point?

Peace isn't for
the times in my life
when all is
hunky dory,
and peachy keen.

No.
Peace is
for the moments
when all of hell
is trying to
break into
my heart.

Peace is to be
the guard
fighting
at the door
of my heart.

Peace needs
to be ready
at all times.

And then,
when the heat is on,
peace needs to
step up and defend.

In these moments
of the battle,

if we are
prepared
and have hidden
God's Word
in our heart
and if we know
that we know
that we know
peace is ours
for the taking
and the living in,
then we simply
need to call
on the power
of the Holy Spirit
and hold our ground.

We are in spiritual warfare.
This is a 24-7 fight.

We cannot
for one moment
let our guard down.

We cannot
for one moment
think we have arrived.

We cannot
take our eyes
off our Jesus
and place them
onto the
"test of life"
placed in
front of us
and expect
to walk away
victorious.

I shouldn't have been
caught off guard.

I am not *ignorant*
of the devil's schemes.
(2 Corinthians 2:11)

I know to
"*Be sober-minded, be alert.*
Your adversary the devil
is prowling around
like a roaring lion,
looking for anyone
He can devour".
(1 Peter 5:8)

I also know my God.

I know that
"*The one who*
is in you
is greater than
the one who
is in the world."
(1 John 4:4)

I know that
"*I can do*
all things
through Christ,
who strengthens me."
(Philippians 4:13) NKJV

I know when
I have a demand
placed on me,
my God will
supply all your needs
according to his riches

in glory in Christ Jesus."
(Philippians 4:19)

I know to
"Don't worry
about anything,
but in everything,
through prayer and petition
with thanksgiving,
present your requests
to God.
And the peace of God,
which surpasses all
understanding,
will guard
your heart and minds
in Christ Jesus."
(Philippians 4:6-7)

I know,
I know,
I know.

Now,
it is time
to live it.

Time to
apply it.
Time to
make it work
in my life.

I know this
is not the last
pop quiz
that will
come my way.

The Testing Times of Life

Somewhere,
sometime,
when I am least
expecting it,
I will be tested again.

The next time,
I pray
I stand
in the peace
I know to be mine.

I pray
I use my
sword of the spirit
and defeat
the enemy of my soul.

I pray
I master the art
of living in the spirit
and living in peace.

What about you?
Has your peace
been tested
this week?

Remember,
our God is faithful.

If you think
you are
standing strong,
be careful not to fall.
The temptations
in your life
are no different
from what others experience.

265

And God is faithful.
He will not allow
the temptation
to be more than
you can stand.
When you are tempted,
he will show you
a way out
so that you can endure.
~1 Corinthians 10:12-13, NLT

Life is all
about learning
how to live it.

Thankfully,
in Christ,
we are able
to sit
at the feet
of the Master teacher.

Yes, indeed.
"...he knows
the way I have taken;
when he has tested me,
I will emerge as pure gold."
~Job 23:10

Big Mouths and Little Ears

For eighteen years,
when I got
out of bed
in the morning
and went to work,
it was to a place where
little hearts and minds
looked up to me
as "teacher".

This was a title
I always prized,
and yet at times,
felt so unworthy of.

For with this title
came the utmost
responsibility
to mold young lives
not only for life
in this world,
but also for eternity.

When I stood
before my class,
it was Jesus
I wanted them to see.

267

Yet so many times,
I got in the way,
or should I say,
my big mouth did.

I was made
humbly aware
of the tremendous
influence
I had on my students,
each time I would hear
words I'd spoken
coming out
of *their* mouths.

Words of impatience.
Words of condemnation.
Words of disappointment.
Words of hurt.

It was quite obvious
I had a big mouth
and their little ears
were listening!

The Bible tells us
the tongue
is the smallest member
of the body,
and yet
the hardest to control.

How true this is.

Yet, knowing
that the power
of life and death
are in the tongue,
we so carelessly

Big Mouths and Little Ears

enter into conversation.

We speak first
and think second,
if we bother
to think at all.

How we like Paul
need to pray
our words
will always be
seasoned with grace
and will be edifying
to all ears,
especially little ones.

Like David,
our prayer should be
that the Lord
would set a guard
before our mouths.

As Christians,
we need to realize
our words
not only condition
the hearts
of those
who hear them,
but also reveal
for all to see,
the spiritual condition
of our own heart.

An unhealthy mouth
is merely a symptom
of a spiritually
unhealthy heart.

It was Jesus himself
who diagnosed
this life-threatening illness
in Matthew 12:34 -
"For the mouth speaks
from the overflow
of the heart."

Our words
are a reflection
of our heart
and our only hope
is found
in a new heart.

In Ezekiel 11:19
God promises
to take
our stony heart
and replace it
with a heart of flesh.

A heart that is
tender,
compassionate
and keenly aware
of the words
that flow forth
from it.

As a teacher,
and most importantly
as a Christian,
I need
this new heart.

I need to sit
at the feet of Jesus
each day

Big Mouths and Little Ears

learning anew
His language of love.

A language
that speaks life
to the hearer.

Words of affirmation.
Words of encouragement.
Words of dignity and praise.
Words of hope.

What were my words
really saying
to those precious little ones
who had been entrusted
to my care?

What are your words
saying to those
in your
sphere of influence?

What kind of heart
is touching theirs?

If ever in doubt,
we need simply
to listen
to our mouth
and it will tell us.

Remember,
even if our own ears
aren't listening
to the words
we are speaking,
we can be certain,
plenty of other ears are!

The Want To

His answer
was simple enough.

Or, was it?

A couple
of weeks ago,
as I was
driving home
from work,
I hit the
scan button
on my radio.

A few short
seconds later
I found myself
eavesdropping
on a conversation
between two gentlemen.

I had landed
on this station
just in time
to hear
the host
of this radio show
ask the following question:
"So what kind

of qualifications
does one need
in order to succeed
in your line of work?"

The man
being interviewed
simply responded,
"the want to".

I was hooked.

I quickly reached
for the scan button again.
They had my
complete attention.

The interview continued
and so did my curiosity.

As I listened,
I speculated about
what occupation
they might be
referring to.

Imagine my
surprise
when I finally
figured out
what this man
did for a living.

Any guesses?

According
to this gentleman,
If you have
the "want to",

you, too,
can become a.........
drum roll, please...........
professional rodeo clown!

I had to smile.

Of all the
occupations
that had
popped into
my mind,
I have to admit
professional rodeo clown
was not one of them.

But then,
it all started
to come into focus.

Having the
"want to"
made perfect sense.

I have a feeling
if this radio host
had been interviewing
any one of the
twelve disciples,
they, too
may have
responded
with the exact
same answer.

*Walking along
the beach of Lake Galilee,
Jesus saw two brothers:
Simon (later called Peter)*

and Andrew.
They were fishing,
throwing their nets
into the lake.

It was their regular work.

As he was walking along
the Sea of Galilee,
He saw two brothers,
Simon (who is called Peter),
and his brother Andrew.
They were casting
a net into the sea -
for they were fisherman.

"Follow me,"
He told them,
"And I will make you
fish for people."
Immediately
they left their nets
and followed him.
~Matthew 4:18-20

After this,
Jesus went out
and saw a tax collector
named Levi
sitting at the tax office,
and he said to him,
"Follow me."

So,
leaving everything behind,
he got up and began
to follow him.
~Luke 5:27-28

Were any of
these men
qualified
to be a disciple
of the Most High God?

What did they
themselves
even know
about God?

How could they
possibly lead
others to God?

And yet,
Jesus called
them into service
and they took Him
up on His invitation.

They had
the "want to"
and that was
all they needed.

What about you?
What about me?

Over my lifetime,
I have passed up
many God-given
invitations
simply because
I felt I was
unqualified?

I have a
feeling

you have, too.

Like me,
you have
probably heard
the voice of Jesus
calling you
to follow Him
into a new place,
a new career,
a new direction,
a new life...
and yet,
you opted
to stay put,
right where you were.

You may still
be in this same,
seemingly "safe"
spot today.

The disciples
could easily
have talked
themselves
out of this
new calling.

After all,
they already
had an occupation.

They were
already
knee-deep
in their livelihood.

They knew
how to fish
and they were
good at it.

Matthew not only
knew how to
collect taxes
for the government,
but for his
own pocket,
as well.

They weren't
listening
for the knock
of opportunity.

They weren't
looking to
"find themselves".

They weren't
looking
for God.

Yet,
when
the knock came
and the door
to a new life
in Christ
was opened
before them,
they took the
leap of faith
and jumped
in with both feet.

The Want To

They were caught....
hook,
line
and sinker.

Why?

Because they were qualified?

No.
Simply because
they had
the want to.

The Jesus
who gave them
the invitation
of a lifetime
is still the Jesus
who calls out
to you today.

He is still
looking
for people
to walk away from
all that they know,
all that they do,
and follow Him.

When Jesus calls you,
He is not looking
at your qualifications.

The one who
created you
knows better
than you
what you were

created to do.

The one
who formed you
in your mother's womb
knows better than you
that for which
you were formed.

Jesus is still calling today.

He is still giving
you and me
the invitation
of a lifetime.

He is still
knocking on the
doors of our hearts
and presenting us
with the opportunity
to stand in the gap
for those
in our arena of life.

Are you willing
to say "yes"?

Are you willing
to leave it all
behind
and follow Him?

If so,
all you have
to have is
the "want to".

God's Sweet Spot

I will never
forget the day
little Chris
taught us all
how to hit a baseball.

Chris was in
first grade,
but that didn't
stop him
from being
the best batter
out on the field.

It was morning recess
and the diamond
was filled
with children
of various ages
and grade levels.

The players
had been
divvied up,
the teams
were in place,
and the game
was in full swing,
and so was Chris.

As soon as
the first ball
was thrown
in his direction,
the bat,
a mere extension
of his arm,
met it and whack!

The ball
sailed over
the fence
and Chris
trotted around
the bases.

As he made
his way across
home plate
another student
called out,
 "WOW!
How did you do that?"

"Easy,"
came Chris's reply.
"I found the sweet spot."

Ahhhhhhh...
the sweet spot.

The one place
on the bat....
where....
when the
ball and bat connect...
home runs are inevitable
and smiles are undeniable.

God's Sweet Spot

Today,
I discovered
the sweet spot.

No,
I haven't been
out on the field
trying my luck
at one of America's
favorite pastimes.

Where I have been
is right where God
has called me to be.

Have you
ever wondered
if you are in
God's will?

I think we all
have grappled
with this question
at least once
in our lifetime,
if not
on a regular basis?

As followers
of Christ
we want
nothing less
than to be
smack dab
in the center
of God's will.

We know God
has a plan

for our life
and we don't
want to miss it.

We want
to know
that we know
that we know
we are right
where we should be.

Today, I knew.

This day was
no different
than any other day.

I woke up,
went to work,
came home,
and now,
here I am
sitting on my couch,
writing.

Just
another day
in the life of Stacy.

Yet, today,
I hit
a spiritual
home run.

As I went
through this
ordinary day,
doing ordinary things,
I felt the extraordinary

God's Sweet Spot

peace of God
flood over me.

All day,
and in every way,
I knew
that I knew
I was right
where God
would have me
to be.

God's will
for my life
and my desire
to follow Him
in His purpose
for my life
connected.

Like a baseball
and a bat,
the two made contact.

 I found the sweet spot.

But wait,
you say.
I don't get it.
You just said today
was an ordinary day.

What makes you
so sure
you found
the sweet spot?

How did you
know

*you were in
God's will?*

How does
a batter
know
he found
the sweet spot
on the bat?

He hears the sound.

He feels the jolt.

He sees the ball
heading out of the park.

Today,
in my innermost being,
I heard the sound
of God's approval.

Today,
in my innermost being,
I felt the jolt
of God's power
working in me
and through me.

Today,
I saw God's
purpose
being fulfilled
before my very eyes.

*And so,
dear brothers and sisters,
I plead with you
to give your bodies*

God's Sweet Spot

to God
because of all
he has done for you.

Let them be
a living
and holy sacrifice—
the kind
he will find acceptable.
This is truly
the way
to worship him.

Don't copy
the behavior
and customs
of this world,
but let God
transform you
into a new person
by changing
the way you think.

Then you
will learn to know
God's will for you,
which is good
and pleasing
and perfect.
~Romans 12:1-2, NLT

My sweet spot.
It's not my job.
It's not my marriage.
It's not where I live.
It is my life.

The whole of it.

The way I live it
each and every day.
It is losing
myself in Christ,
and allowing Christ
to be found in me.

This is God's will.

This is my sweet spot.

To Chris,
there was
no mystery
to knowing
how to hit
a home run.

It was simply
a matter
of making
a connection.

When you find
the sweet spot,
it just happens...
naturally
and triumphantly.

It is the same with us.

When our life
finally connects
with Christ;
when the creator
of the universe
and the one
He created
finally come in

complete contact
one with another,
God's will just happens....
supernaturally
and gloriously!

Ahhhhhhh...
God's sweet spot.

The one place
in your life....
where....
when God's will
and your desire
connect...
the abundant life
is inevitable
and the smile
of your heart,
undeniable.

Out of the Box Living

I've spent most
of my life
crammed inside
a box.

Rules.
Expectations.
Status quo.
Formalities.
Legalism.

Uhgghh.....
just talking
about these
confining walls
makes me feel
as though
I am suffocating!

Oh...
I see you
shaking your head
and nodding
right along with me.

You are familiar
with box living, too.

Out of the Box Living

Anyone who has
been in the box
knows exactly
what I am
talking about.

Boxed-in living will kill you.

It will suck
what little life
you have
right out of you.

As long as
you make
your abode
inside the walls
of performance,
you will find
yourself
gasping for air.

LEGALISM!

Living by
the letter
of the law
rather than the spirit.

Thankfully,
I have been
set free.

God's grace.
God's marvelous grace
knocked down
the walls
and set me free.

And the more time
I spend with Jesus
the freer I become.

"Are you tired?
Worn out?
Burned out on religion?
Come to me.
Get away with me
and you'll recover your life.
I'll show you how
to take a real rest.
Walk with me
and work with me—
watch how I do it.
Learn the unforced
rhythms of grace.
I won't lay
anything heavy
or ill-fitting
on you.

Keep company with me
and you'll learn to live
freely and lightly."
~ Matthew 11:28-30, MSG

Now, I am living!

I am
inhaling
and exhaling.

I am
flexing
and bending.

I am
moving

and shaking.

I am alive.

Life is not
a rigid set
of rules
and regulations.

Life is not
a list of do's
and don'ts.

Life is not
a checklist
of things
to accomplish.

Life is not
governed
by the ticking
of a clock.

Life is not
staying
inside the lines!

Life is ebb and flow.
Life is come and go.
Life is this and that.
Life is living and breathing and changing.

Living in the
box of legalism
will kill you.

Trying to live
by the letter
of the law

just brings death.

We can't.
We aren't able.
We were not made to.

Living outside
the box,
by allowing God
to live inside of you,
will bring life.

Beautiful life.
Abundant Life.

The kind of life
Christ thought
was worth
dying for
to give
to you and me.

When we live
by the spirit
of the law,
by surrendering
to God's spirit
at work in us
and through us,
God can.
God is able.
God accomplishes
that for which
we were created
to accomplish.

Are you still
in the box?

Out of the Box Living

Are you still
gasping for breath,
struggling to live?

Take hold of God's grace.
Grab onto His love.
Accept His forgiveness.

Invite Him
to move
into your heart
and into your life.

Get out
of the way
and let God
have His perfect way
in your will
and in your life.

Breathe in His spirit
and watch it
knock down
the confining walls
of your life.

Life is meant
to be lived,
and true life
is found
in none other
than Christ Jesus.

I have come
so that
they may have life
and have it in
abundance.
~John 10:10b

I am finally
and completely
out of the box
and there is
no way
I am ever
going back.

What about you?

Life in a box..............
or...............
life in Christ.

Praise God!
I see your walls
starting to topple!

Just Do It

In order to
be successful
at something,
we must be
willing
to give it
100%.

At least,
that's what
we have been
taught, right?

Recently,
however,
I read
an article
with a rather
unusual twist.

According
to the author,
most people try
to jump in
with both feet,
giving the proverbial 100%,
only to give up
and abandon ship
altogether.

He encouraged readers
to instead
start with 10%.

He then went
on to highlight
the difference
a mere 10%
could make
in regards
to ones health.

Take losing weight,
for example.

Instead of
setting your goal
on the ultimate
amount of weight
you would like
to lose,
he suggests
focusing
on losing 10%
of your total body weight.

If you weigh 160,
set your goal
to lose 10%,
or 16 pounds.

By doing this,
your weight
would drop to 144!

That's a significant difference!

Or,
how about

getting
adequate sleep?

If you are
currently getting
seven hours
of sleep at night,
he suggests crawling
under the covers
forty minutes earlier
each evening.

This would amount
to around 10%
more sleep a week.

Think of the
extra energy
and productivity
you would gain
by making
this small change.

Do you suffer with
high blood pressure?

Try reducing
your daily salt intake
by 10% and
see what happens.

The author
went on
to list
seven more changes,
that when given
only 10%,
would pay
huge dividends

in a person's
overall health.

As I read
the article,
I found myself
nodding my head
and thinking,
"Yeah, I could do *that.*"

Somehow,
only focusing
on 10%
made these changes
seem more doable.

They no longer
felt out
of my reach,
but rather
right
at my fingertips.

I immediately began
to formulate
a plan
to begin making
some of these
new lifestyle changes.

You know what they say.
If we fail to plan,
we can plan on failing.

But planning
is not enough.
In order
to be successful,
I am actually

going to have to
implement my plan.

This is true
for any change
we desire in our life.

The finish line
will never
be reached
if we aren't
first
willing to start
moving
in that direction.

In essence,
the author
of the article
was simply saying this:
start doing something,
even if that something
is very small.

Getting started
is definitely
the hardest part.

I know for me
personally,
it's the beginning
that usually
keeps me
from beginning
as strange
as that may
sound and be.

There are
so many things
I should be doing,
yet they remain undone.

I just can never
seem to get
started
and that's why
the article I read
caught my attention.

Maybe the
whole reason
I don't start is
I am looking
at the big picture.

While that
in itself
is not a bad thing,
it can prove
to be intimidating enough
to keep
you and me
frozen in our tracks.

Starting small
seems like
a logical
starting point
to me.

Zerubbabel must
of thought so, too:

After that,
the Word of God
came to me:

*"Zerubbabel started
rebuilding this Temple
and he will
complete it.
That will be
your confirmation
that God-of-the-Angel-Armies
sent me to you.*

*Does anyone
dare despise
this day
of small beginnings?
They'll change
their tune
when they see
Zerubbabel setting
the last stone in place!"*
~ Zechariah 4:8-10, MSG

Today,
what are you
putting off
until tomorrow?

What changes
have you been
wanting to make
but haven't?

What pounds
need to be lost?

What devotions
need to be written?

What clutter
needs to be removed?

What classes
need to be taken?

What debts
need to be paid?

What dreams
live in your heart
but still have yet
to be birthed
into reality?

Come on!

Let's do it!...
and let's start today!

God Knows Where You Are

Have you ever
wondered
if you have
fallen off
God's radar?

Life was merrily
rolling along
and then
all of a sudden
you found yourself
in a prison,
out to pasture,
thrown in a tomb.

Joseph.
David.
Lazarus.
You.
Me.

No matter
where you are.
No matter
how silent you
find this place to be.

Rest assured.

God knows where you are.

He has not forgotten you.

You are not out of His sight.

In fact,
chances are,
where you are
is right in the center
of God's will.

When only a youth,
God gave Joseph
a glimpse
of where he would
one day be.

Prison wasn't it.

In fact,
his journey to prison
was nothing
Joseph could ever
have imagined.

From a pit,
to slavery,
to prison.

Where was God in this?
Right beside Joseph,
that's where.
Waiting for the
perfect,
God-ordained time
to take Joseph's hand
and lead him
from the prison

right into the palace.

David was out
in the pasture
tending sheep
when Samuel
came calling
with a call from the Lord.

His family may
have overlooked him.
His own father may
not have thought him
worth calling for.

But God hadn't
forgotten about him.

In fact,
David was the reason
Samuel had come.
He was God's man
and soon
everyone knew it.

The shepherd
soon became King.

And then
there was Lazarus.
Sick, dead,
and buried,
but far
from being forgotten.

Jesus came
and not a minute
too soon.

He was right
on time and Lazarus
received a call
of his own.
At the words of Christ,
life came into his body
and he came forth,
out into the light
of God's resurrection power.

So, what about me?
What about you?

Maybe where you are
is far from where
you ever thought
you would be.

Looking around your life,
you, yourself,
have doubts
as to where
you even are.

Don't worry.
God knows where you are.

In His perfect timing
and in His perfect way,
He will come calling.

He sees you
in the prison.
He is with you
in the lonely pasture.
And yes,
even in the
dead places of your life,
the places where you

can no longer see
a sign of life,
He is there.

Stay faithful to your calling.

Stay faithful to your God.

Keep trusting Him
in these dark,
barren places
of your life.

He is with you.
He is working
behind the scenes
and one day,
it will happen.

The door will open.
The call will come.
The dead will spring forth with life.

As Joseph stood
before his brothers,
the very ones
who had sold him
into slavery,
he proclaimed this truth.

You intended to harm me,
but God intended it all for good.
He brought me to this position
so I could save the lives of many people.
~ Genesis 50:20, NLT

God's purpose was revealed.

HEARTPRINTS OF GOD – The Early Years

David,
who had been
faithful to keep
a watchful eye
upon his father's sheep,
was now the one
being gazed upon
as Samuel anointed him
to tend the sheep of Israel.

God's purpose was revealed.

Lazarus,
dead, buried,
and lifeless
for four days,
walked right out
of the tomb
and back into the lives
of everyone watching;
a living testimony
of God's power
to bring
whatever is dead
back to life.

Lazarus walked
in newness of life
and once again,
God's purpose was revealed.

The God of
Joseph,
David,
and Lazarus
is our God, too.

When it seems
God has forgotten us

or life has taken
a wrong turn,
we simply need
to remember this:
God has a purpose.

Where you are
is not a mistake.

The place you
find yourself
is not off God's radar.

If you will but
surrender to
God's call on your life,
everything you are
currently going through
can be used
by God
to prepare you
for your final destination.

Soon,
in God's
perfect timing
and in His
perfect way,
He will come calling.

Soon,
His purpose
will be revealed
in your life, too!

God's Heart of Love

One morning,
before I left
for work,
I lovingly
placed a
small, red
plastic heart
in the coffeemaker.

Yes,
you read
that right.....
the coffeemaker.

I pulled out
the container
normally reserved
for the filter
and the coffee,
and placed
"my heart"
there instead.

As I walked away
from the kitchen
and headed
out the door,
I couldn't help
but smile

God's Heart of Love

as I thought
of the surprised look
sure to be
on my husband's face
when he made
coffee
later that morning.

Before the coffeemaker,
the red heart
had been spotted
when,
one evening,
I returned home
from work
to find a
beautiful flowering
potted plant
sitting on our
bathroom window sill.

The heart
was propped up
against the purple pot,
in plain sight
for all to see.

Before the plant,
the red heart
had surprised
my husband
when,
one morning
he bent down
to pick up
the newspaper.

Both the heart
and the morning news

313

were waiting
to greet him
on the sidewalk
leading
to our home.

Before this,
I had discovered
the heart
in the refrigerator,
atop a container
of leftovers
I had planned
to take
for my lunch
that day.

The heart exchange
is something
my husband and I do
on a regular basis.

It was never
discussed
or planned,
it just happened.

We have been
doing it
for so long,
I'm not sure
how it actually
got started,
but it has yet
to lose its "magic".

The heart
is a symbol
of our love

314

God's Heart of Love

for each other,
and I'm not sure
which is
more rewarding -
leaving the heart
to be found,
or discovering it!

As I tucked
the heart
into the coffeemaker,
I thought
about God
and the beautiful
and faithful way
He, too,
tucks reminders
of His love
into each
of our days.

Sometimes,
God's love
is seen
in the obvious,
like the
beautiful
flowering plant,
showcasing His love
for all to see.

Other times,
however,
His heart
may be tucked
into the mundane,
day to day places
of our lives
like the refrigerator

or the coffeemaker.

In every situation
and in every place,
God's love
is waiting
to be discovered.

In a beautiful sunrise.

In a baby's laugh.

In a promotion.

In a good meal.

These are the
obvious places.
Yet God's love
is also found
in the not
so obvious.

In the dark of night.

In the tears of suffering.

In failure.

In times of desperation.

In the
refrigerator times
of life,
when all
seems cold
and we are
shaking with fear,
God's love is there.

God's Heart of Love

In the
coffeemaker times
of life,
when the
stress
and demands
of day to day living
cause us to
percolate and steep
in the heat
of the battle,
God's love is there.

God's love
is even
waiting for us
when we
receive news
that leaves us
uncertain
of the future.

If we just look,
we will see His heart.

Last night,
with a wink
and a smile,
my husband
informed me
his morning coffee
was the best
he had ever had.

That was
my intention:
to sweeten
his day
with a

reminder
of my love for him.

Today,
keep your
eyes open
for reminders
of God's love
for you,
and this day
just might
turn out to be
the best *today*
you've ever had!

About the Author~

Stacy is a seeker of God's heart.
Daily she is learning who she is
in and through Christ Jesus, her Lord.
She is a heart transformed by His love,
a life changed by His presence,
a sinner saved by His grace.
As she seeks
to know God more intimately,
through the ordinary,
day to day happenings of her life,
she marvels to discover
God is always faithful
to leave heartprints of His love
scattered across the pages
of her life story.
It is these heartprints
Stacy writes about on her blog,
"Heartprints of God",
and loves to speak about
at women's events.

It is the desire of Stacy's heart,
that through the sharing
of her own heartprint of God sightings,
others will start to see
heartprints of God

in their own lives
and be drawn ever closer to Him.

Stacy prays
that as the Holy Spirit
speaks through something she writes,
or something she says,
others will find God,
and in doing so,
find the very heart
of who they are.

Stacy - a teacher of 18 years -
is currently a writer, and speaker.

Connect with Stacy~

Stacy loves recounting
God's faithfulness in her life
and sharing His heartprints.
For weekly heartprint sightings,
subscribe to her blog at
stacylsanchez.com

On social media follow Stacy on
Facebook, Instagram, and Twitter
at Heartprints of God.

Stacy is also available
to speak at women's events and retreats.
If you're interested
in having Stacy come
to your event
email Stacy at stacy@stacylsanchez.com

Made in United States
North Haven, CT
09 August 2023

40160407R00195